BRIDGE FOR BRIGHT BEGINNERS

by
Terence Reese

DOVER PUBLICATIONS, INC.
NEW YORK

This Dover edition, first published in 1973, is an
unabridged and unaltered republication of the
work originally published in 1964. This edition is
published by special arrangement with Sterling Pub-
lishing Company, Inc., 419 Park Avenue South, New
York, New York 10016, publisher of the original
edition.

Library of Congress Catalog Card Number: 73-77446

International Standard Book Number

ISBN-13: 978-0-486-22942-3
ISBN-10: 0-486-22942-4

Manufactured in the United States by Courier Corporation
22942422
www.doverpublications.com

Contents

1. About Cards and Tricks

"Oh, if only I had time to learn to play bridge!" Of course you have time. You can get the feel of this game inside half an hour!

To play a real game, you need cards, a table, score-pads, four chairs, and three friends to play with. In a pinch you can dispense with the table, the score-pads, and the friends. You can begin (as I did) by dealing out a deck of cards on the carpet.

How the cards and suits rank

Sort the cards, as we say, into suits, so that they look like this:

> Spades (♠)
> Ace King Queen Jack 10 9 8 7 6 5 4 3 2
> Hearts (♡)
> Ace King Queen Jack 10 9 8 7 6 5 4 3 2
> Diamonds (♢)
> Ace King Queen Jack 10 9 8 7 6 5 4 3 2
> Clubs (♣)
> Ace King Queen Jack 10 9 8 7 6 5 4 3 2

There are 13 cards in each of the four suits. These lines show how they rank in bridge. That is to say, the Ace is a better card than the King, the King than the Queen, and so on. The order is not difficult to remember, except perhaps that the Ace counts high. You would expect the King to rank higher than the Queen, and of course the Jack (or Knave, as it is sometimes called) ranks below the throne.

The five top cards, Ace King Queen Jack Ten, are called HONORS. They possess no special magic in the play, but in certain circumstances you score a bonus simply for holding honors.

We have put the suits in order, too—spades, hearts, diamonds, and clubs. The suits rank this way, spades better than hearts, etc., but that will not concern us in the first two chapters.

There were two reasons why I asked you to lay out a deck of cards in this fashion. One was that you would see how the cards (and suits) rank in bridge; the other so that, with the 52 cards sorted into suits, you could easily pick them out and reproduce the deal below. For you are going to play a hand of bridge right now!

First, look at the North hand in the diagram and pick out the cards you want. Set this opposite to yourself, for you are going to be South. Then pick out the West hand, followed by the East hand. If you haven't made any mistakes so far, the thirteen cards left will form the South hand.

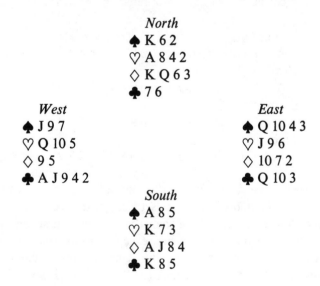

North
♠ K 6 2
♡ A 8 4 2
◇ K Q 6 3
♣ 7 6

West
♠ J 9 7
♡ Q 10 5
◇ 9 5
♣ A J 9 4 2

East
♠ Q 10 4 3
♡ J 9 6
◇ 10 7 2
♣ Q 10 3

South
♠ A 8 5
♡ K 7 3
◇ A J 8 4
♣ K 8 5

Now that you have set out the deal in this fashion, with the cards in a suit going from left to right, I want you to change each layout or hand so that the cards actually lie like this:

North

♠	♡	♢	♣
K	A	K	7
6	8	Q	6
2	4	6	
	2	3	

In writing, we use the horizontal form, because it is easier to read as the eye travels across. When you are actually laying the cards out to play, the vertical arrangement is more convenient.

I should add that North, South, East and West are not meaningful terms in an actual game of bridge where the players all have names. They are simply used for convenience in writing, to designate the players. North and South are partners, playing against the partnership of East and West.

One other point: You will find that you can pick out the cards more readily if the BLACK and RED SUITS are arranged alternately in your hand. Most players do sort their cards like that, and so should you. It makes no difference, however, so long as you pick from the right suit when you play a card.

The first trick

Now we can begin. You, South, are the man at the wheel, known in bridge as the DECLARER. (In written bridge hands, you will almost always find that South is the declarer.) The opponent on your left, West, makes the first play or LEAD by putting a card face up in the middle of the table. Let us say that he leads the 4 of clubs, which would be a sound choice from his hand. Now you have to play a card from North's, your partner's, hand opposite. The rules of the game require that a player must, if possible, contribute a card of the same suit as has been led. You have therefore the "choice" between the 7 and 6. These cards are in effect the same, being next to one another in rank, so you play the 6. East plays next, and he puts on his highest club, the Queen. You have a still higher club, the King, and you play it.

That completes the first TRICK. You have played the highest card, the King, so you have won the trick. You collect the four cards and turn them face downward in front of you.

Quite a simple operation, but you have already learned the meaning of three important terms in bridge: declarer, lead and trick. Add one more to your stock: the players on the other side, East and West when you are South, are called the DE-FENDERS, and play the DEFENSE.

Tricks two to nine

You have won the first trick with the King of clubs. What next? It doesn't matter a lot on this hand, but your eye will probably be caught by the diamonds, where you and North between you hold all the top cards. Because you won the last trick in your hand, you have the privilege of making the next lead and you choose the Ace of diamonds. West plays the 5. As you have already played a winning card, there is no point in putting on the King or Queen from North, your partner's hand. You play the 3. In the same way it would be pointless for East to contribute one of his higher cards. He plays the 2.

That's the second trick won by your side. You gather the cards again, turn them over, and lay them across the first trick. It is your lead again, for you played the winning card.

Trick 3—Continuing diamonds, you play the 4 and this time win in the North hand with the King. West plays the 9 and East the 7.

Trick 4—Now North has the lead. You play the 3 of diamonds from North, East plays the 10, and you (South) the Jack, making sure that you win the trick. West has no more diamonds, so he has to play a card of another suit. This is called DIS-CARDING. As he may hope to win tricks sooner or later with his clubs, West discards the 7 of spades.

Trick 5—You lead your fourth diamond, the 8, towards North's Queen. West discards the 5 of hearts this time, and East the 3 of spades.

Trick 6—You still do not wish to surrender the lead because you know that the defenders have several clubs to make as soon as they come in to lead them. You lead the 2 of hearts from North and play the King. You know that this must win because the Ace—the only card to beat the King—is held by North. East plays the 6 of hearts on this trick and West the 10. (Remember that West has already discarded one heart.)

Trick 7—You are still "in" (on lead) with the King of hearts, so you lead the 3. West must play his last heart, the Queen; the North hand plays the Ace, and East the 9.

Trick 8—You have two more certain tricks, the King and Ace of spades. From North you lead the King of spades, East plays the 4, you the 3, and West the 9.

Trick 9—The 2 of spades is led from North to your Ace. East plays the 10 and West the Jack.

Tricks ten to thirteen

You have won the first nine tricks and there are four cards left in each hand. As you can see, you have no chance of making any more tricks, for East has the best spade, the Queen, and the best heart, the Jack. If you lead either suit, East will win the trick and then CASH his other high card. Then he will lead a club, and West will win the last two tricks with his high clubs. If, instead, you should lead a club at the tenth trick, West will win the last four tricks himself.

Remember what we said earlier, that you could get the feel of this game inside half an hour? Already you have played a complete hand with thirteen tricks. What is more, on this particular hand a world champion could not have made more tricks than you did!

2. Ways of Winning Tricks

When you played the hand in the first chapter you made all but one of your tricks with cards that were sure winners from the first. The exception was the King of clubs. This became a winner because the opponent on your left LED AWAY FROM his Ace of clubs.

Forcing out high cards

Some hands go like that, but mostly there is a battle between the two sides to ESTABLISH tricks. Imagine that the spade suit is distributed about the table in this way:

North

♠ K 10 4 3

West   *East*

♠ 8 7   ♠ A 9 6 5

South

♠ Q J 2

We assume, as usual, that South is the declarer. No matter who leads a spade, the defense can take the first trick if they wish to. After that, North-South win the next three tricks. If South were starting this suit, he would lead the Queen, West would play the 7, and North the 3. East might take his Ace immediately or he might play low, knowing that the Ace can win only once. If East plays the 5, South continues with the Jack. Say now that East plays the Ace. When North-South regain the lead they make two more tricks with the ESTABLISHED King and 10.

Here is a typical deal in which both sides strive to establish their long suits. We suggest that you set out the cards again, for in the early stages you will find it easier to follow the play with cards than in the diagram. But that won't be so for long: You will soon find it as easy to read a diagram as a line of print.

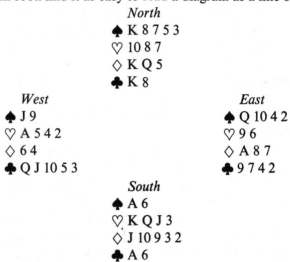

North
♠ K 8 7 5 3
♡ 10 8 7
♢ K Q 5
♣ K 8

West
♠ J 9
♡ A 5 4 2
♢ 6 4
♣ Q J 10 5 3

East
♠ Q 10 4 2
♡ 9 6
♢ A 8 7
♣ 9 7 4 2

South
♠ A 6
♡ K Q J 3
♢ J 10 9 3 2
♣ A 6

As South is declarer, West has to make the first or OPENING LEAD. It would not be good play to start with the Ace of hearts. That would be like spending a week's pocket money the first day and going hungry for the rest of the week. Instead of releasing this high card, West will begin with his longest suit. His correct choice is the Queen of clubs.

You, the declarer, have two sure winners in clubs, the Ace in the South hand and the King in the North. It is not always right by any means to play winning cards at once, but here it would not be an astute move to play the 8 from North and the 6 from your own hand. If you did that, the King and Ace would fall together on the next round, and you would end up with one trick in the suit instead of two. It is not important here whether you win the first trick with the King or the Ace. Let us say that you play the King from North and low from your own hand.

15

Now if you were being pursued by devils you could take three more tricks quickly with the Ace and King of spades, and the Ace of clubs, but that wouldn't be good play at all. You might make one or two more tricks at the finish, but you wouldn't be making the best of the hand.

Just as it was right for West to start on his long club suit, so you should set about establishing the best suit held by your side. Given time, you could develop tricks in spades, hearts or diamonds. But you are not going to have time, for the opponents have a long suit of clubs which they are going to RUN as soon as they have forced out your Ace. So you ask yourself, "In which suit can I develop the most tricks?"

Spades are the poorest prospect. You have two top winners, but you cannot be sure of establishing any lower spades quickly. In hearts, once you have forced out the Ace, you are sure of three tricks. In diamonds, you can expect to take four tricks, so the diamonds have it.

You lead the King of diamonds from North. East may take this at once with the Ace so that he can continue the clubs, which his partner has led. The second trick is therefore won by East. At the third trick he leads a club and, of course, your Ace of clubs wins.

Now you run off your diamond tricks. In an actual game you must watch the opponents' discards rather closely when they can no longer follow suit. If several spades are THROWN OFF, you will look for extra tricks for yourself in that suit. If they discard their clubs, you might have time to establish some hearts.

As the cards lie, East-West are not likely to be embarrassed in their discards. West, who will have to discard three times on diamond leads, can conveniently let go three small hearts. East will have no temptation to UNGUARD the spades by throwing the 2 and 4.

Suppose, then, that when you have finished leading diamonds, no clubs have been discarded by West and not more than one spade by East. Three tricks in clubs and the Ace of hearts are the very least that the opponents will make if you LET THEM IN the lead. You cannot do better than make your Ace and King of spades. That will give you eight tricks—all that was possible against good defense.

This should teach you an important lesson. Bridge is a game of thoughtful planning and intelligent strategy—not just a matter of leading out Aces and Kings.

Winning tricks with low cards

As you will have noticed already, low cards often win tricks as well as high cards. Whenever you hold a long suit, you can expect to develop tricks by playing out top cards and extracting those of the opponents. Imagine a spade suit divided as follows:

North
♠ K Q 7 4 3

West   *East*
♠ 10 8 5   ♠ J 9

South
♠ A 6 2

South begins with only three certain winners, the Ace, King and Queen. He plays off the Ace and both opponents follow suit. Already South can be sure of at least one extra trick. Remember that there are always THIRTEEN in a suit. You and North hold eight spades, so the opponents hold five. Even if the three spades outstanding after the first round are in the same hand, North will have more spades than anyone else and his fifth spade will be established in time. As it happens, both opponents follow suit again when a low spade is led to the King. With only one spade now outstanding, North can be sure of three more tricks from his Q 7 4.

In the next example, the extra tricks are developed after one round has been given up to the opponents:

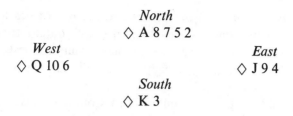

North
◇ A 8 7 5 2

West
◇ Q 10 6

East
◇ J 9 4

South
◇ K 3

Here North-South begin with only two sure tricks. If it were South's unlucky day—if one opponent held five diamonds—two tricks might be all. When both opponents follow to the King and then the Ace, prospects brighten. A third round is played from North, and declarer's best hopes are fulfilled when the suit BREAKS 3 – 3. That leaves North with two master cards.

Establishment of tricks in this way occurs on almost every deal and we shall see many more examples. What I want you to note is that LENGTH in a suit is an advantage just as much as STRENGTH. To give an extreme example, if you had a suit of ten cards headed by the Ace and 10, and your partner held the SINGLETON (lone) Jack, you might make ten tricks in it even though you were missing the King and Queen. So when, in the next two chapters, we attempt to judge the value of a hand, we count for length as well as for high cards.

The meaning of a trump suit

In the two hands that you have played so far, the suits were all equal in power and value. That is to say, if you had the lead and played the 2 of clubs, and no one else had a club left to play, it would be your trick.

I have a surprise for you. Most hands are not played under those conditions. One suit usually has superior rank over the others, and this suit is called the TRUMP SUIT. The cards in it are called TRUMPS. The word *trump* is thought to be a corruption of *triumph*, and the trump suit does indeed triumph over the others.

Suppose that spades are trumps. The Ace of clubs is led by West and North and East follow suit with lower clubs. Now if South has a club he must follow suit as well, but if he has none he can win the trick by playing *any* spade, even the 2. David knocks out Goliath.

As you can imagine, the existence of a trump suit makes a big difference to the course of play. Here is a simple example:

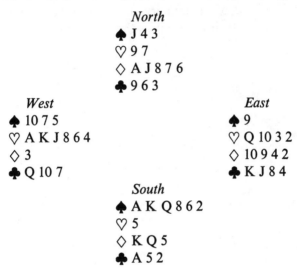

North
♠ J 4 3
♡ 9 7
♢ A J 8 7 6
♣ 9 6 3

West
♠ 10 7 5
♡ A K J 8 6 4
♢ 3
♣ Q 10 7

East
♠ 9
♡ Q 10 3 2
♢ 10 9 4 2
♣ K J 8 4

South
♠ A K Q 8 6 2
♡ 5
♢ K Q 5
♣ A 5 2

Suppose first that the hand were played like those we have already played, with no trump suit. West would lead one of his top hearts and the defenders would make the first six tricks, all in hearts.

Now let us say that spades were trumps, as in actual play they would be. Again West leads the King of hearts and follows with the Ace. But South, having no more hearts, will trump this second trick by playing a spade. He will then play out three rounds of spades in order to DRAW THE TRUMPS of his opponents. Five diamonds follow and the Ace of clubs, making a total of twelve tricks for South when he plays the hand in spades.

Finally, can you picture West as declarer, playing with hearts as trumps? He can make as many as ten tricks, losing only one spade trick (for East can trump the second round), one diamond and one club.

So you see that when you have a long suit, and your partner has some cards in it as well, it helps a lot to play with that as the trump suit. The bidding process described in the next chapter is a kind of preliminary skirmish in which both sides seek to establish their long suit as the trump suit.

3. Preliminaries and the Bidding

We are going back a little, now, to see what happens when four people sit down at a card table for a game of bridge. The first thing to decide is who is going to play with whom. Unless there is a previous arrangement, the four players CUT for partners by spreading the cards face downward across the table and drawing a card apiece. The two highest play against the two lowest. As between equal cards, the rank of suits is the determining factor.

The pair which cuts the high cards has the choice of seats and also of cards. (It is usual, though not essential, to use two decks of cards for alternate deals.)

The player who cuts the highest card deals the first hand. The deck that he has chosen is given to the player on his left to shuffle. It is then passed across to the dealer's right-hand opponent for him to cut. The dealer passes out all the cards one by one, starting with the player on his left and ending with himself. During the deal his partner shuffles the deck not in use and places it on his own right, ready for the player to his right to deal the next hand. Thus the position of the second deck always indicates the dealer.

The players now pick up their cards and sort them into suits, holding them close to the chest, so that they are not seen by the other players. Then the bidding begins.

The meaning of a contract

Before we describe what happens in the BIDDING, you must understand its purpose. The bidding determines three things: whether the hand is to be played with no trump or with a particular suit as trumps; who is to be the declarer, playing both his own cards and his partner's cards; and how many tricks he must make to fulfil his CONTRACT. Every hand is played in a contract of one sort or another, with one side undertaking to make a specified number of tricks either at no trump or with a particular suit as trumps.

Just as an auction starts with a bid of a certain minimum amount ("Will anyone bid me twenty dollars for this valuable clock?"), so the most modest bid at bridge is to make seven of the thirteen tricks. A player who offers to make seven tricks with clubs as trumps does not say "Seven Clubs," however, but "One Club." When he calls "One Club" it is understood that he contracts to make seven tricks, for the declarer must always make the first six tricks, known as THE BOOK, before his tricks start counting towards the number he has contracted for.

One Club is the lowest contract in which a hand can be played. The highest bid is Seven No Trump. That would be a contract to make all thirteen tricks with no trump suit. The denomination of NO TRUMP ranks above spades, the highest suit, so Seven No Trump is a higher contract than Seven Spades.

The third point that the bidding settles is who should be the declarer. This privilege goes to the partner who *first* mentioned the suit of the final contract. Suppose that North and South reach a contract of Four Spades, which would be a contract to win ten tricks with spades as trumps. If North was the first player to bid spades, then he would play the hand as declarer. If South had mentioned spades first, then he would be declarer, even if North actually made the final bid of Four Spades.

The bidding

You realize now what the players are trying to do when they bid. Each partnership is trying to arrive at a contract that suits its combined hands. As the bidding proceeds, the partners build up a picture of one another's holdings and estimate how many tricks they can make at No Trump or in their best suit. At the same time they listen in to the messages exchanged by their opponents.

Now we can pass on to the procedure in bidding, also called THE AUCTION. South, the dealer, makes the first call. He can either pass, which means that he makes no promises, or he can, in theory, bid anything from One Club upwards. Except on rare hands of a special type, the early bids are generally at a low level, as at any auction.

As the bidding proceeds, each player calling in turn, the only rule is that each new bid must be at a higher level than the previous CALL or bid. Either it must be for more tricks, or for the same number of tricks as the last bid but in a higher denomination. Let us say that the bidding begins:

South	West	North	East
1♠	2♣	2♡	pass
3♡	pass	?	

We read, as usual, from left to right. South, having a long suit of spades, opens the bidding with One Spade. This is technically a contract to make seven tricks with spades as trumps, but the auction seldom ends with a low call of this sort. West, who bids next, has a club suit. He cannot call One Club, for that is a lower call than One Spade, so he makes the lowest legitimate call in his suit, Two Clubs. Now North RESPONDS to his partner's opening bid, and shows that he has strength and length in hearts by bidding Two Hearts.

East, in fourth position, has nothing to say and passes. South has support for his partner's suit and REBIDS with a RAISE to Three Hearts. West passes, and now if North and East pass too, the bidding will be over and the final contract will be Three Hearts. Although South made the bid of Three Hearts, his partner was the one who called hearts first, and North would be the declarer.

Double and redouble

You may wonder why, since West had a good club suit, he did not bid higher in clubs to prevent the opponent from playing the hand in hearts. Well, you don't make a bid at any auction for an item you can't afford to buy. In bridge, if you attempt to play in a contract that is higher than you can manage, and you do not win as many tricks as you have contracted for, you incur a penalty. You have to consider this when you bid.

This brings us to another type of call, the DOUBLE. A player who judges that his opponents have bid beyond their limit can increase the penalties by doubling. Of course, the double also increases the reward for making the contract, if declarer should succeed. A double has no effect on the level of the bidding. That is to say, if Four Clubs is doubled, the next higher call is Four Diamonds, just as when Four Clubs has not been doubled.

A player whose side has been doubled can REDOUBLE, increasing the penalty for failure, as well as the reward for success, still further. This again does not affect the level of the bidding. Here is an auction containing more than one double and redouble:

South	West	North	East
—	1♡	2♣	double
pass	pass	2◇	2NT
pass	3NT	pass	pass
double	pass	pass	redouble
pass	pass	pass	

West has dealt this hand and he opens the bidding with One

Heart. North overcalls with Two Clubs. Now East, who holds some clubs and knows that his partner holds some strength since he opened the bidding, is confident that North cannot make his contract of Two Clubs, so he doubles. After two passes North rescues himself into Two Diamonds, his second suit. Evidently East also holds diamonds, for he bids Two No Trump now and is raised by his partner to Three No Trump. At this point South decides that his opponents are out of their depth, so he doubles. But East daringly redoubles. Everyone passes and the hand is played in Three No Trump redoubled, promising plenty of excitement for everybody.

The opening lead

As perhaps you noticed when you played the two earlier hands, the opening lead is always made by the player on the left of the declarer. After he places a card face up on the table, everyone gets a chance to see the DUMMY.

Declarer and dummy

As soon as the opening lead has been made, the declarer's partner lays all of his cards face upwards on the table. He arranges them in suits, and if the hand is being played in a suit contract he places the trumps on his right. The hand he puts down is the dummy, and he likewise is called dummy. As befits a dummy, he must remain silent and take no part in the play. He is allowed to draw attention to an irregularity, or prevent his partner from committing an irregularity. Such an irregularity might be leading from the wrong hand or failing to follow suit.

The declarer has to play from both hands, but it would be wrong to suppose that his task is more difficult than that of the defenders. For the most part, it is easier to play as declarer with dummy than to defend.

Game and rubber

The next thing to learn is how to score a game. When you make your contract, each trick (over six—the book) scores a certain number of points. At No Trump the first trick over book counts 40 points, and each succeeding trick counts 30. If the contract is in spades or hearts, called the MAJOR SUITS, each trick scores 30. In diamonds and clubs, the MINOR SUITS, each trick is worth 20 points.

To make game you have to score 100 points. This means that Three No Trump bid and made (40 + 30 + 30) will give you GAME. You need to bid and make Four of a major suit (4 × 30) or Five of a minor suit (5 × 20) for a game. It is obviously easier to make a game in a major than a minor suit.

You can also make game in two or more steps. Say that on the first deal you bid One No Trump and make eight tricks. You score 40 towards game for the one-trick contract bid and made. The extra trick counts 30 points, but this is scored in a different place and does not count towards game. The 40 is called a PART SCORE. If on a later hand you make a contract worth 60 or more you have scored a game—provided always that the opponents have not made a game in the meanwhile. If your opponents reach game first, your part score retains its value in points but does not contribute towards the next game. It is WIPED OUT.

The first side to win two games wins the RUBBER. Winning the rubber carries a big BONUS, so making game is an important objective, like winning a set in a tennis match. Remember these GAME CONTRACTS:

> Three No Trump
> Four Spades—Four Hearts
> Five Diamonds—Five Clubs

The value of game has a big effect on the bidding. If you are not going to try for game in spades, for example, you may as well play in Two Spades as in Three Spades. But if you can make ten tricks it is essential to bid Four Spades, for if you bid only Three Spades and make an overtrick you will not score a game. You get credit towards game only for the number of tricks you bid (and make).

Small and grand slams

Other landmarks in the bidding are a contract for twelve tricks, which is a SMALL SLAM; and for thirteen tricks, a GRAND SLAM. A small slam is worth approximately twice as much as a game, and a grand slam twice as much again as a small slam. Of course it does not pay to bid slams recklessly. If you contract for Six Spades and fall a trick short you have thrown away an easy game. As a beginner, you will need to be fairly sure of your ground before you embark on a slam contract.

A throw-in

There is one further situation in bidding that we must mention. As the next chapter will show, certain standards are required for opening the bidding, and sometimes none of the players will want to open. When there are no bids (four passes) the hand is THROWN IN or PASSED OUT and the deal passes to the next player in the usual way.

The rest of the scoring

It is not necessary, while you are learning the game, to understand all the scoring. All you need to know at this stage is that certain contracts—for game or slam—are important objectives in bidding. Full details of the scoring are given in chapter 11.

4. When to Open the Bidding

Bidding is a partnership enterprise, with the partners building on one another's calls until they reach a contract that expresses their combined values. The process starts with the OPENING BID.

Point count

A player who opens with a bid of One in a suit or of 1NT tells his partner that he has better than an average hand in terms of high cards. There is a popular system of valuation for high cards, called POINT COUNT:

Ace   = 4 points
King   = 3 points
Queen = 2 points
Jack   = 1 point

Opening One of a suit

If the high cards in a deal were distributed equally to all the players, each would hold one Ace, one King, one Queen, and one Jack. That would be a total of 10 points, an average hand. To open the bidding with One of a suit you require, as a minimum, about 13 points when you have no LONG SUIT (five cards or more); 12 points when you hold a five-card suit; and 11 points when you hold a good six-card suit or two five-card suits. Let us look at some examples.

$$
\begin{array}{lll}
(1) & \spadesuit \text{ K J 10 8 7 6 4} & = 4 \text{ points} \\
& \heartsuit \text{ 10 5 4} & = 0 \text{ points} \\
& \diamondsuit \text{ 2} & = 0 \text{ points} \\
& \clubsuit \text{ Q 3} & = 2 \text{ points}
\end{array}
$$

You may think this is quite a useful hand played in spades. I am glad you see it like that, because it shows you appreciate the value of long suits. However, there is a good reason why this is not a sound opening bid. It does not contain enough support for any call in another suit that your partner might want to make. When you OPEN you say to him, not only that you hold a biddable suit, but that you hold some high cards that will be useful in *any* contract. On the first round you should pass this hand. If partner opens, then you are free to RESPOND with a bid in spades.

$$
\begin{array}{lll}
(2) & \spadesuit \text{ 7 5 2} & = 0 \text{ points} \\
& \heartsuit \text{ A J 8 4} & = 5 \text{ points} \\
& \diamondsuit \text{ K 7} & = 3 \text{ points} \\
& \clubsuit \text{ K Q 6 3} & = 5 \text{ points}
\end{array}
$$

Now you have no suit to compare with the spades in the last example, but you hold 13 points. That means that you should look for an opening bid of some kind. You have two possible suits, hearts and clubs, both of four cards. One Club, keeping the bidding low, is preferable to One Heart on this minimum hand.

In the next example one suit is longer than the other:

$$
\begin{array}{lll}
(3) & \spadesuit \text{ 7} & = 0 \text{ points} \\
& \heartsuit \text{ A J 8 5 3} & = 5 \text{ points} \\
& \diamondsuit \text{ K Q 6 2} & = 5 \text{ points} \\
& \clubsuit \text{ K 7 4} & = 3 \text{ points}
\end{array}
$$

The general rule is to open the longer suit. Thus the bid on this hand is One Heart.

We look next at some hands where the main strength lies in the long suits rather than in the high cards:

(4)	♠ A Q 10 8 4	= 6 points
	♡ K J 9 7 4	= 4 points
	◇ J 10 5	= 1 point
	♣ —	= 0 points

Only 11 points, but two good major suits. With two five-card suits, open the higher, One Spade. Then it will be convenient to show your hearts on the next round. If partner prefers spades he will later be able to put you back to spades without raising the level of the bidding.

Here the virtue lies in just one good suit:

(5)	♠ A 8	= 4 points
	♡ 9 7 4 3	= 0 points
	◇ 2	= 0 points
	♣ A Q J 10 8 6	= 7 points

A sound opening of One Club, for you have two Aces and a particularly good suit containing four honors. If the hand is eventually played in clubs the honors will score a bonus (see page 83), and you can take this into account.

Very good hands, counting up to 21 points or more, may also be opened with a bid of One:

(6)	♠ A K 5	= 7 points
	♡ 4 3	= 0 points
	◇ A K 8 5	= 7 points
	♣ A K 4 2	= 7 points

This hand is strong in high cards but it lacks a long suit and you won't make a game unless partner can respond to your bid of One. Open One Diamond, the higher of your four-card suits.

(7) ♠ K Q J 4   = 6 points
      ♡ A Q J 2   = 7 points
      ◇ 6   = 0 points
      ♣ A K J 3   = 8 points

Again a bid of One is sufficient. On strong hands like this, as on most weak hands, the lowest of three four-card suits tends to be the best opening because it leaves plenty of space in which the bidding can develop. Open One Club, leaving partner room to respond One Diamond on quite a weak hand. As soon as you hear from him you will set your sights on game, if not slam.

Some hands raise a problem because you feel that they are worth an opening bid, yet there is no good suit:

(8) ♠ 10 6 5 2   = 0 points
      ♡ A 8 3   = 4 points
      ◇ K Q 6   = 5 points
      ♣ A J 2   = 5 points

With 14 points you can hardly pass, for that might lead to a throw-in and a missed game. Your only four-card suit is very weak. On such occasions it is advisable to open with a minor suit rather than a major. Bid One Club, although you have only three clubs. Partner will not raise you high in clubs unless he has five or more. Remember that to make game in a minor you have to make eleven tricks, whereas nine tricks are sufficient for game in No Trump, and ten for a game in a major suit. An opening bid in a minor suit is often just a way of approaching a no-trump contract.

Opening 1 NT

The last hand we looked at, example (8), would be described as a BALANCED HAND, because the distribution was even and there were values of a sort in every suit. Somewhat stronger balanced hands, counting about 16 to 18 points, are opened

One No Trump. Suppose that we add the Queen of spades in place of a small spade, so that the hand becomes:

$$
\begin{array}{lll}
(9) & \spadesuit \text{ Q 10 6 2} & = 2 \text{ points} \\
& \heartsuit \text{ A 8 3} & = 4 \text{ points} \\
& \diamondsuit \text{ K Q 6} & = 5 \text{ points} \\
& \clubsuit \text{ A J 2} & = 5 \text{ points}
\end{array}
$$

This would be a typical, though minimum, One No Trump opening. The next example is a maximum:

$$
\begin{array}{lll}
(10) & \spadesuit \text{ A Q 7} & = 6 \text{ points} \\
& \heartsuit \text{ K J 10 4} & = 4 \text{ points} \\
& \diamondsuit \text{ K 9} & = 3 \text{ points} \\
& \clubsuit \text{ A J 8 2} & = 5 \text{ points}
\end{array}
$$

It would not be a fatal mistake to open One Heart or One Club, but, with honors in every suit, One No Trump describes the hand more accurately.

It is quite in order to open One No Trump with a five-card suit, especially a five-card minor, so long as you have the general strength (16 to 18 points) and no suit is weaker than K x or J x x. (The symbol x is used to describe any low card.)

$$
\begin{array}{lll}
(11) & \spadesuit \text{ K 9 4} & = 3 \text{ points} \\
& \heartsuit \text{ A 10} & = 4 \text{ points} \\
& \diamondsuit \text{ A J 6} & = 5 \text{ points} \\
& \clubsuit \text{ K Q 10 6 3} & = 5 \text{ points}
\end{array}
$$

Again One Club would not be a mistake, but One No Trump gives the whole picture in a single bid.

Higher opening bids

You have noted that opening bids of One cover a wide range. The great majority of openings are at this level. Hands that are exceptionally strong in high cards or powerful in distribution may be opened with a higher call. Opening bids of more than One are described in chapters 9 and 10.

5. Responses to an Opening Bid of One

The partner of an opening bidder is called the RESPONDER, and his bids are RESPONSES. Using the language of bridge, responder tries to tell the OPENER about his hand—how much strength he has and where the strength lies.

When your partner has opened the bidding you must bear in mind that he may well be hoping for another chance to bid. He may be strong, and ready for game if you can help a little, or he may have a second suit to show. In general, you aim to give your partner a chance to bid again, but on some hands, containing not more than 5 points with no support for partner and no good suit of your own, you must pass. For example, partner has opened One Spade and you hold:

(1) ♠ 6 3
♡ Q 6 4 2
♢ K 5 3
♣ 8 7 4 3

Only 5 points and a weak hand in every respect. If partner had a maximum there might just be a game, but it is unsound to make that assumption. You should pass.

The decision is unpleasant when you are very short in your partner's suit. He opens One Heart and you hold:

(2) ♠ 7 5 4
♡ —
♢ Q 8 7 6 3 2
♣ Q 10 5 2

You don't like leaving him in One Heart, but to call anything else is dangerous. Two Diamonds might be a better final contract than One Heart, but you will not be able to stop there. If he has support for diamonds he will carry you too high. Still worse, he may repeat his hearts, and then the opponents may be in a position to double. You must take your medicine and pass One Heart. There is always a chance that the opponents may enter the bidding and give your partner another chance to bid.

When to respond 1NT

One No Trump is the standard response on moderate balanced hands containing about 6 to 9 points. You would respond One No Trump to any bid of One, including One Club, on a hand like this:

(3) ♠ Q 10 5
♡ J 8 7
◇ K 7 5
♣ J 6 4 2

One No Trump is often the right response even when you hold a five-card suit:

(4) ♠ J 6
♡ K 8 7 4 2
◇ Q 7 5
♣ 10 4 2

Over One Spade, respond One No Trump, rather than Two Hearts. Over One Diamond or One Club you would respond One Heart.

Sometimes you may respond One No Trump with slightly more than the usual maximum of 9 points:

(5) ♠ 6 4 3
♡ Q 7 4 2
◇ A J 5
♣ K 6 3

The only sensible response to One Spade is One No Trump.

Responding in partner's suit

When you hold four or more cards in the suit that your partner has opened, it is generally a good move to support him by raising the bid in his suit, especially if your hand is weak. Distribution of responder's hand is an important factor, however. Compare these two hands in response to partner's opening of One Spade.

(6) ♠ Q 10 8 4   (7) ♠ 10 8 4 3
    ♡ 5   ♡ J 5 2
    ◊ Q 8 7 5 2   ◊ K 8 7 3
    ♣ K 6 3   ♣ K J

Hand (7) contains more points, but hand (6) is the stronger of the two in support of spades. This is partly because the spades themselves are higher, but more because hand (6) contains a singleton (the 5 of hearts), and extra tricks can be made in the play by trumping heart leads. Hand (6) has a fair SIDE SUIT as well (the diamonds).

The better the distribution, the fewer points you need for a single raise in partner's suit:

(8) ♠ J 10 7 4 2
    ♡ —
    ◊ 10 8 6 4 3
    ♣ 9 5 2

Only 1 high card point, but it is correct to raise One Spade to Two Spades, or One Diamond to Two Diamonds, because of the length of those suits and the BLANK or VOID in hearts.

You can also raise a major suit with only three trumps, but you will need from about 6 to 9 points:

(9) ♠ K 7 4
    ♡ 8 3
    ◊ 10 7 4 2
    ♣ A 8 5 3

Raise One Spade to Two Spades.

A double raise in partner's suit

We turn now to a response that is still short of game but nevertheless extends promise of game. This is a double raise, from One Heart to Three Hearts, or One Diamond to Three Diamonds, etc. Such bids are forcing. A FORCING BID is one which the partner *must not pass*. Even if he has a minimum for his bid, he must KEEP THE BIDDING OPEN by calling again.

A rough standard for a double raise is 11 points with four trumps and a singleton, or 13 points with four trumps and a DOUBLETON (a suit of two cards).

(10) ♠ 6
♡ K J 8 4
◊ Q J 7 4 2
♣ A 10 5

You have a sound double raise of partner's One Heart or One Diamond.

(11) ♠ K J 6 3
♡ J 2
◊ A Q 6 4
♣ K J 5

This hand, in support of spades, is much stronger in high cards than the last example. It is not too strong, however, for the response of Three Spades. Remember that this is forcing, so there is no danger of stopping short and missing game. Partner will bid Four Spades if his opening was no better than minimum. If he thinks there is a possibility of slam he will encourage you by bidding another suit, and you will accept the invitation.

Over partner's opening of One Diamond you have the values for Three Diamonds, but an EXPLORATORY or APPROACH BID of One Spade would be a better choice. It is a long way to go to game at Five Diamonds, and this hand may well play better in Three No Trump. If partner can rebid One No Trump over your response of One Spade you will go straight to game by bidding Three No Trump.

Response of 2NT

This is another strong response, forcing to game. The average needed is equivalent to an opening bid—13 to 14 points—and a balanced distribution, with some strength in all the other three suits.

(12) ♠ K J 4
♡ Q J 9
◇ A Q 3
♣ J 9 6 2

With the above hand, respond Two No Trump to any opening bid of One, including One Club.

(13) ♠ J 4
♡ Q 10 9 5
◇ A K 6
♣ K 10 8 2

Here you would respond Two No Trump to an opening One Spade, but over One Club or One Diamond you would approach with One Heart, rejecting Two No Trump because of your weakness in spades. This response in a new suit is FORCING FOR ONE ROUND (that is, partner must bid at least once again).

You will note that there is quite a gap between the responses of One No Trump (6 to 9 points) and Two No Trump (13 to 14 points). On intermediate hands, the usual procedure is to make a simple response in a new suit and follow with Two No Trump or Three No Trump on a later round.

A new suit at the level of One

The responses that we have examined up to now have all had a fairly narrow range. When you respond One No Trump or Two No Trump to partner's opening bid, or give him a single or double raise, he knows within fair limits the value of your hand. A change of suit has a much wider range, from 5 points up to about 17.

$$(14) \quad \spadesuit \; 6\,3$$
$$\heartsuit \; K\,J\,9\,6\,4$$
$$\diamondsuit \; J\,7\,4\,2$$
$$\clubsuit \; 5\,3$$

With only 5 points it would be advisable to pass over One Spade, but over One Club you could respond One Heart. Of course, this hand is much weaker than, say, example (13), where you also responded One Heart to One Club. Don't worry about that. Partner will bid again and you will have another opportunity to express your values. On this hand (14) you will naturally pass on the next round unless partner makes a forcing rebid, demanding that you keep the bidding alive.

When you hold a TWO-SUITER in response to partner's opening, the general rule is to bid the longer suit first, or, when they are of equal length, the higher ranking.

$$(15) \quad \spadesuit \; A\,Q\,6\,2 \qquad (16) \quad \spadesuit \; K\,9\,7\,4\,3$$
$$\heartsuit \; K\,10\,8\,4\,3 \qquad \qquad \heartsuit \; A\,K\,7\,4\,2$$
$$\diamondsuit \; J\,7 \qquad \qquad \qquad \diamondsuit \; 7$$
$$\clubsuit \; 5\,2 \qquad \qquad \qquad \clubsuit \; Q\,3$$

Over One Diamond or One Club respond One Heart on hand (15) as you have five hearts and only four spades. On hand (16) respond One Spade (the higher-ranking of two equal-length suits) even though the hearts are headed by the Ace-King.

Responding at the level of Two

A response in a new suit at the level of Two promises upwards of 9 points, or slightly less if you have a six-card suit. It is forcing for one round, so you must not make this bid on too weak a hand. You may recall an earlier example:

(17) ♠ J 6
♡ K 8 7 4 2
◇ Q 7 5
♣ 10 4 2

You noticed that over One Spade it would not be sound to respond Two Hearts, although you could properly bid One Heart over One of a minor.

This is the type of hand on which you can slightly lower the standards:

(18) ♠ Q 3
♡ 4
◇ K Q J 9 7 6
♣ 10 8 4 2

With so good a suit you cannot come to much harm if you give a POSITIVE RESPONSE of Two Diamonds to partner's One Spade or One Heart.

Responses at game level

A response of Three No Trump to an opening bid is similar in character to a response of Two No Trump, but with higher point count—the standard being about 15 to 16 points.

(19) ♠ K 7 4
♡ A J 5
◇ K 10 8 4
♣ K Q 9

The above is a typical response of 3NT to any opening bid of One. Note the balanced distribution and the honors in every suit.

A direct jump to game in partner's suit, One Heart—Four Hearts, or One Club—Five Clubs, tends to be based on distribution rather than on high cards:

(20) ♠ Q 10 8 7 3
♡ —
◇ K J 9 5 4 2
♣ 6 3

Over One Spade jump straight to Four Spades. One of the objects of the call is to SHUT OUT the opponents from the bidding. The next player to speak may hold a big hand, but he may not think it safe for him to enter the bidding at such a high level.

Jump bids in a new suit

The strongest call you can make in answer to your partner's opening is a jump—one more than is necessary—in a new suit. The strength required is usually about 18 points. This can be shaded to 16 when you hold a very strong suit of your own or exceptional support for the suit that partner has opened.

(21) ♠ A K 10 4
♡ A 8
◇ K Q 3
♣ K 7 4 3

With the above, jump to Two Spades over a bid of One Club, One Diamond or One Heart. Over One Spade, respond Three Clubs. This JUMP SHIFT is a FORCE TO GAME. Both players must keep the bidding open until game (at least) is reached.

(22) ♠ 6 2
♡ A K J 10 7 4
◇ A Q 6
♣ Q 7

Force with Two Hearts over One Diamond or One Club. Your partner is hardly likely to open One Heart when you hold six, including four honors. To force over One Spade you would have to bid Three Hearts. However, Two Hearts, forcing for the moment, would be sufficient.

The requirements can be lowered when you have good support for your partner's suit:

(23) ♠ 6
♡ A Q 8 4
◇ A K 7 5 2
♣ Q 10 5

You would bid only Two Diamonds over One Spade, but over One Heart you can force with Three Diamonds. On the next round, of course, you will show your support for partner's hearts.

Responses to 1NT

Responses to One No Trump are easier than to One of a suit because you have a better picture already of partner's strength. He will have from 16 to 18 points and balanced distribution. In general—and this is an important figure to remember—25 points in the two hands will afford a play for game in Three No Trump. With 9 points you can raise to Three No Trump, for you know that the combined minimum is 25. With 8 points you can raise to Two No Trump. With 7 points you are on the borderline and will be guided by your holding of good intermediate cards like 10's and 9's.

(24) ♠ 7 4 2   (25) ♠ Q 5
♡ A K 5   ♡ 10 9 7 3
◇ 8 6 5 3   ◇ K 9 6 3
♣ 8 4 2   ♣ Q 8 7

Hand (24) is about as bad as a 7-point hand could be, for there are no 10's or 9's and all the points are in one suit. You would pass 1NT without hesitation. On hand (25) you have a sound raise to Two No Trump.

Unbalanced hands, containing a singleton, may play better in a suit contract, and you will have to judge whether to make a simple response at the level of Two, not forcing, or a jump response, forcing to game.

(26) ♠ J 9 7 5 3 2   (27) ♠ Q J 10 7 4
     ♡ K 4 2   ♡ 4
     ◇ 6   ◇ A 9 5 3
     ♣ 5 4 3   ♣ J 5 2

On hand (26) you would take out One No Trump into Two Spades. On hand (27), with 8 points and a good suit, you would force to game with Three Spades, and your partner will go on to Four Spades, knowing where your length lies, or Three No Trump if he thinks he can control the other suits.

Stayman convention

There is one specialized response to One No Trump that we must mention because you will surely meet it as soon as you go out into the wide world—the STAYMAN CONVENTION. A convention in bridge is an agreement to use a particular bid in an artificial sense. In the Stayman Convention a response of Two Clubs to One No Trump does not mean, "I have a suit of clubs," but asks, "*Do you hold four cards in either major suit?*" Say that partner opens One No Trump and you hold:

(28) ♠ A 9 6 4
     ♡ J 8 5 3
     ◇ 3
     ♣ Q J 6 3

Prospects of game at No Trump are doubtful, but if partner holds four cards in either spades or hearts, you might well make game in the suit. Playing in hearts or spades you would control the diamonds—a likely weakness at No Trump—and would be able to take tricks with small trumps by RUFFING (trumping).

Over One No Trump, therefore, you respond Two Clubs, asking partner to bid a four-card major suit if he has one. If he has not, he will bid Two Diamonds artificially. On hand (28) you will raise to Three if partner bids either major. Over Two Diamonds you will bid Two No Trump.

This convention can be equally useful when you hold only one of the majors:

(29) ♠ 6 3 2
♡ A J 8 5
♢ K J 7 4 2
♣ 10

Now you intend to reach game, but game in hearts will be safer if partner holds four hearts. You respond Two Clubs, intending to raise Two Hearts to Four Hearts. If partner rebids Two Spades or Two Diamonds you will bid Three No Trump, trusting him to hold the clubs.

Responding after a pass

Throughout this chapter we have assumed that you as responder have not already passed. When you have already passed and then respond to partner's third- or fourth-hand opening, your bids are qualified by the original pass, and promise less strength than the requirements for a non-passed hand. Simple changes of suit in this case are not forcing. A jump in a new suit is forcing and implies a fit for the suit that has been opened. Other seemingly strong responses, such as a double raise and Two No Trump, are qualified by your original pass and are not forcing. The range for Two No Trump by a passed hand is about 11 to 12½.

Summary of responses

We have covered a lot of ground in this chapter, and you may like to review the different types of response to partner's opening bid.

Over an opening bid of One in a suit

Pass	With less than 6 points, unless you have a good suit that can be called at the level of One, or good support for partner's suit.
1NT	Moderate balanced hand, 6 to 9 points.
Single raise	Moderate support, usually between 3 to 9 points, at least Q x x or four small cards in partner's suit, and a short suit outside.
Double raise	Four cards in partner's suit, about 11 points with a singleton, or 13 points with a doubleton. Forcing to game.
2NT	Useful balanced hand, about 13 to 14 points. Forcing to game.
New suit at level of One	Wide range, from about 5 points to 17. Forcing for one round.
New suit at level of Two	Usually from about 9 to 17 points. Forcing for one round.
3NT	Balanced 15 to 16 points.
Raise to game	Mainly distributional, usually five trumps and a singleton or void (blank suit).
Jump in new suit	Unlimited strength with about 18 points upwards, but may be less with good support for partner's suit. Forcing to game.

Over an opening 1NT

Pass	Up to about 6 points, with no long suit.
Two of a suit	Up to about 6 points, with a long suit and a singleton.
2NT	8 points or a *good* 7.
3NT	Upwards of 9 points.
Three of a suit	About 8 points with a five-card suit, possibly less with a six-card suit or two five-card suits. Forcing to game.
Two Clubs	Stayman Convention, asking partner to bid his four-card major, if he has one.

After you have passed at first opportunity

A simple bid of a new suit is not forcing. A jump in a new suit is forcing and implies a fit for opener's suit.

6. The Play at No Trump

We return to the play now that you can follow the bidding and understand the meaning of a contract. Here is a deal that shows many aspects of the play at No Trump:

North
♠ 8 6
♡ 7 5 2
◇ A 10 8 4
♣ A 7 4 3

West
♠ K 9 7 3 2
♡ Q 10 4
◇ J 3 2
♣ 10 8

East
♠ Q J 4
♡ A J 8 3
◇ 9 7
♣ J 9 6 2

South
♠ A 10 5
♡ K 9 6
◇ K Q 6 5
♣ K Q 5

South is the dealer and makes the first call. A balanced hand, with 17 points: what does that suggest? Right, an opening bid of One No Trump.

West passes and North has to respond. Eight points. Is that enough for a raise to Two No Trump?

Remember the figure 25, which normally is enough for Three No Trump. The opener should hold between 16 and 18, so at worst there will be 24 points in the two hands, at best 26.

North, with 8 points, can suggest game by raising to Two No Trump. South, who has a point better than minimum, accepts the INVITATION and bids Three No Trump. So the bidding goes:

South	West	North	East
1NT	pass	2NT	pass
3NT	pass	pass	pass

Hold-up play

Trick 1. West, on the left of the declarer, leads from his long suit, spades. It is usual against a No Trump contract to lead the fourth highest card, which in this case would be the 3. Declarer plays the 6 from dummy, and East plays the Jack. The general rule with touching cards, like the Queen and Jack in this instance, is to *lead* the higher card but to *play* the lower card.

South has only one GUARD (winning card) in spades. In No Trump contracts it is usual to hold up such a winning card for as long as possible, so South plays the 5. The reason for that play will appear later on.

Trick 2. Having won the first trick with the Jack of spades, East follows with the Queen of spades, playing to establish his partner's suit. South again holds up his Ace, playing the 10. West, of course, plays low.

Trick 3. East plays his third spade, forcing South to play the Ace. A low heart is discarded from North, the dummy.

Tricks 4 to 7. Now South wins four tricks in diamonds. When both defenders follow to the King and Queen there is only one diamond left, so declarer knows that the Ace and 10 will both be good. West discards the 4 of hearts, and East the 3 and 8 of hearts.

South has made five tricks already and has three certain winners in clubs. There are six clubs against him, and if they break 3 – 3 the last club in dummy will be established.

Tricks 8 to 10. Declarer plays off King, Queen and Ace of clubs. On the third round West discards another heart. This means that there is still one club outstanding and that dummy's 7 is not a MASTER (the highest outstanding card). You will find it helpful at the start to count the cards as they are played—four clubs on the first round, four on the second, three on the third, and so on; with a little experience you will become so familiar with the commoner divisions that you will know almost by instinct whether a low card has been established.

Trick 11. The clubs having disappointed, South has only one chance for his ninth trick. He must lead up to his King of hearts and hope that East has the Ace of hearts and no more spades. Remember that the defenders have already made two spade tricks and that East has a good club.

South is lucky, for on the lead of the low heart from dummy East plays the Jack and South's King wins the trick.

Tricks 12 and 13. East wins the last two tricks with the Ace of hearts and the Jack of clubs.

I hope you have not missed the importance of declarer's hold-up of the Ace of spades at the beginning of the play? If the first or second spade had been won by South, East would still have had a spade when the heart was led from dummy. Then East would have gone up with the Ace of hearts and led a spade to his partner's hand.

The finesse

The deal you have just played contained another new principle, which you may hardly have noticed. Think about the trick you won with the King of hearts. You won it because the Ace was ON THE RIGHT SIDE for you. If West had held the Ace, SITTING OVER the King, your King would have been a dead duck!

Clearly it pays to LEAD UP TO high cards rather than away from them. That principle is seen in one of the commonest plays in the game, the finesse. Study this combination, held by declarer and dummy:

North

A Q

South

6 4

One sure trick, the Ace. But what about the Queen? It all depends on the position of the King. If you LEAD AWAY from the A Q (leading A or Q), then you will surely lose to the King; but if you play from the South hand towards the A Q you can make two tricks whenever West has the King. If West plays low you FINESSE the Queen. If he plays the King, you win with the Ace naturally. We shall meet many more examples of finesses. In the following deal South takes one losing finesse and refuses to take another:

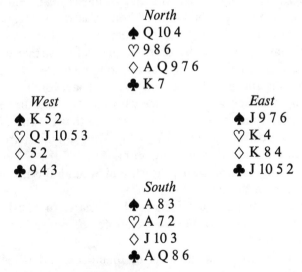

North
♠ Q 10 4
♡ 9 8 6
◇ A Q 9 7 6
♣ K 7

West
♠ K 5 2
♡ Q J 10 5 3
◇ 5 2
♣ 9 4 3

East
♠ J 9 7 6
♡ K 4
◇ K 8 4
♣ J 10 5 2

South
♠ A 8 3
♡ A 7 2
◇ J 10 3
♣ A Q 8 6

Not quite strong enough for One No Trump, South opens One Club. The bidding continues:

South	West	North	East
1♣	pass[1]	1◇	pass
1NT[2]	pass	2NT[3]	pass
3NT[4]	pass	pass	pass

[1]West can almost OVERCALL with One Heart. As we shall see in chapter 9, the defending side can overcall at the range of One on hands that would not justify an opening bid.

[2]This REBID (the usual term for a player's second bid) gives a picture of a balanced hand, not much better than a minimum.

[3]North places his partner with about 13 to 15 points, for he has opened the bidding, obviously on a balanced hand, and has made a LIMITED REBID. North, with 11 points, the King of his partner's suit, and a fair suit of his own, can invite game.

[4]South has a little in reserve, so he is happy to contract for game.

Unblocking

Trick 1. West, obviously, will lead from his heart suit. The usual lead from a combination of honors is the top card, so West chooses the Queen of hearts. Dummy plays low, and now comes an important play by East. He places his partner with a suit headed by the Q J 10 and realizes, looking ahead, that if he plays low the suit may become BLOCKED. (That would happen, for example, if South won at once with the Ace and then gave up a trick to either defender.) To make sure that the run of the suit is not obstructed, East plays the King on his partner's Queen. South plays low, holding up his Ace.

Trick 2. East returns the 4 of hearts and South holds up again. West wins with the 10.

Trick 3. West plays a third round of hearts to CLEAR THE SUIT. East discards a spade (not a club, for he remembers that South bid clubs).

Trick 4. South leads the Jack of diamonds and takes the finesse, playing low from dummy. East holds up his King for one round.

Trick 5. South now leads the 10 of diamonds and tries the finesse again. This time East wins with the King.

Trick 6. East leads the 6 of spades, hoping that his partner will come in to make his good hearts. South could take another finesse by letting this run up to the Queen, but first he counts up his tricks. He can rely on a total of four diamonds, three clubs, and two Aces. It would be foolish to risk the finesse, therefore. South goes up with the Ace of spades.

There is no problem in the rest of the play, except that South could make a silly mistake by leading a high club from his own hand. If he did that, the clubs would become blocked. It is simple enough to take the diamond tricks and then play King of clubs, followed by a low club toward the A Q. Here is a hint that will save you from blocking the run of a suit: first play the high card from the *short* hand.

Ducking

The club combination in the last deal, K x opposite A Q x x, presented a simple exercise in communication. The tricks are there, but declarer must make sure that he is in the right hand at the right time. Such problems are very common. Here the declarer makes use of a manoeuvre known as DUCKING.

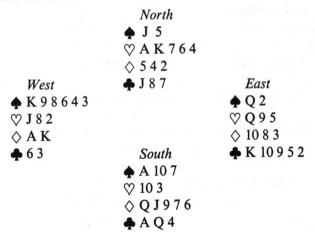

North
♠ J 5
♡ A K 7 6 4
◇ 5 4 2
♣ J 8 7

West
♠ K 9 8 6 4 3
♡ J 8 2
◇ A K
♣ 6 3

East
♠ Q 2
♡ Q 9 5
◇ 10 8 3
♣ K 10 9 5 2

South
♠ A 10 7
♡ 10 3
◇ Q J 9 7 6
♣ A Q 4

South is the dealer and the bidding goes:

South	West	North	East
1◇	1♠	2♡	pass
2NT[1]	pass	pass[2]	pass

[1]South has opened on a minimum, but he has to say something when his partner bids a new suit.

[2]North has nothing in reserve after his first bid. Looking at it another way, North has 9 points and no reason to place his partner with better than a minimum of 13 or so. That is hardly enough for game.

West can judge from South's Two No Trump bid that South has a guard in spades, but no other attack is at all promising.

Trick 1. West leads his fourth best spade, the 6. North plays the 5, East the Queen, and South the Ace. It would be a mistake to hold up with this combination of J x opposite A 10 x, for by killing the Queen with the Ace South ensures two tricks in the suit: the Jack will force the King, and the 10 will be high.

South can be certain of two spade tricks, two heart tricks, and two clubs if he has TIME. To make eight tricks he must develop one of the long suits, either hearts or diamonds. The diamonds may be too slow. As soon as the defenders win with the first high diamond, they will clear the spade suit. If West has led from a six-card suit, which is more than likely as he bid spades on a suit headed by only one honor, the defense will surely take four spades and two diamonds.

What about the hearts, then? Declarer can see seven hearts, which means that there are six out against him. If these divide equally, three in each defending hand, two long hearts can be established. The advantage of playing hearts is that only one trick has to be given up in the process of setting up the suit.

There remains a problem of communication. If declarer plays off Ace, King, and a small heart, he will have no quick ENTRY back to the dummy to make the long hearts. This is overcome by ducking.

Trick 2. South leads the 10 of hearts and ducks in dummy, playing the 4. East wins with the Queen.

Trick 3. East returns his partner's suit, leading the 2 of spades. West wins with the King.

Trick 4. West knows that South has only one spade left, so he plays a third round, won by South's 10.

Trick 5. South plays his second heart to dummy's King.

Trick 6. Now the Ace of hearts is led and South is happy to observe that both opponents follow suit. He knows (and with a little experience will know without needing to count) that the last two hearts are good.

After making the two hearts, South will still need the club finesse to give him eight tricks. With J x x opposite A Q x there is normally no advantage in leading the Jack, for if the next player holds the King he will cover, and the defense will win the third round. South leads a low club from dummy, therefore, and wins two more tricks with the Queen and Ace. He just makes his contract of Two No Trump.

7. The Play in a Suit Contract

Drawing trumps

In suit contracts declarer should always ask himself immediately the question, "Do I draw trumps?" On most hands it is advisable to draw trumps as soon as possible, but sometimes trump leads must be postponed, and sometimes trumps are not drawn at all. The first example is a hand where trumps have to be drawn and the main problem is how to play the trump suit:

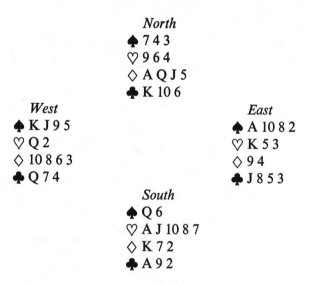

North
♠ 7 4 3
♡ 9 6 4
◇ A Q J 5
♣ K 10 6

West
♠ K J 9 5
♡ Q 2
◇ 10 8 6 3
♣ Q 7 4

East
♠ A 10 8 2
♡ K 5 3
◇ 9 4
♣ J 8 5 3

South
♠ Q 6
♡ A J 10 8 7
◇ K 7 2
♣ A 9 2

South deals and bidding goes:

South	West	North	East
1♡	pass	2◇¹	pass
2♡²	pass	3♡³	pass
4♡⁴	pass	pass	pass

¹This may seem a poor suit for a bid at the level of Two, but remember that a change of suit in response to an opening bid is forcing for one round.

²South has some support for diamonds, and both Three Diamonds and Two No Trumps are possible bids at this point. The simple rebid in hearts is a little weaker than either of those calls.

³Now that the hearts have been rebid, guaranteeing a five-card suit, North has adequate support for a raise.

⁴Having full value for his bids so far, South accepts the game invitation.

With two suits bid against him, West has to choose between spades and clubs for his opening lead. The spades offer better chances of establishing tricks.

Trick 1. West leads the 5 of spades and East wins with the Ace.

Trick 2. East returns a spade, the Queen losing to the King.

Trick 3. West suspects that South has no more spades, but he plays the Jack of spades anyway. South trumps this with the 7 of hearts.

Declarer plans eventually to discard a losing club on dummy's fourth diamond, but first he must draw trumps, or one of the diamonds will be trumped by a defender. The question is how to play the hearts to lose only one trick.

Here we meet a new type of finesse. Declarer will lead twice towards his A J 10 combination, finessing each time. He expects to lose the first finesse but hopes to win the second.

Trick 4. South CROSSES to the Queen of diamonds so that he can play a heart from North.

Trick 5. The 4 of hearts is led from dummy. East plays the 3, South the 10, and West wins with the Queen.

Trick 6. West plays another diamond. (There is no hurry to lead a club, for if his partner has the Ace it cannot be ruffed away.) Declarer wins in dummy with the Jack.

Trick 7. The 9 of hearts is led and successfully finessed.

Now South draws the last trump, makes his King of diamonds, and crosses to the King of clubs so that he can discard his club loser on dummy's last diamond. The contract has been made with the loss of two spades and one heart.

Establishing a side suit

Trumps are often used in the establishment of another suit. Watch how South develops a trick in clubs on the following deal:

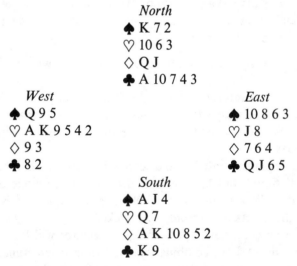

North
♠ K 7 2
♡ 10 6 3
♢ Q J
♣ A 10 7 4 3

West
♠ Q 9 5
♡ A K 9 5 4 2
♢ 9 3
♣ 8 2

East
♠ 10 8 6 3
♡ J 8
♢ 7 6 4
♣ Q J 6 5

South
♠ A J 4
♡ Q 7
♢ A K 10 8 5 2
♣ K 9

North deals and the bidding goes:

South	West	North	East
—	—	pass	pass
1♢	1♡	2♣	pass
3♢	pass	4♢	pass
5♢	pass	pass	pass

In most situations the higher of touching honors is led, but from A K the conventional lead against a suit contract is the King.

Trick 1. West leads the King of hearts. Placing his partner with A K, East drops the Jack. This unnecessarily high card is an encouraging signal. On this occasion East wants to tell his partner that he has a doubleton and can trump the third round.

Trick 2. West leads the Ace of hearts.

Trick 3. When South's Queen falls under the Ace, West knows that dummy's 10 of hearts is a master and also that neither East nor South has any more hearts. In such circumstances it is usually good play to KILL THE WINNER in dummy. West plays a third heart, therefore. East trumps with the 6 and South overtrumps with the 8.

Trick 4. South plays a low diamond to dummy's Jack.

Trick 5. Declarer sees that he has a possible loser in spades. He could try a finesse of the Jack of spades, but a better plan is to seek to establish an extra club trick. Dummy's entry cards must be preserved, so at trick 5 declarer plays the 3 of clubs to his King.

Trick 6. Now he leads the 9 of clubs to dummy's Ace.

Trick 7. A low club is led from dummy and South trumps with the 10 for safety, as he does not want to risk being overtrumped by West's 9 of diamonds.

Trick 8. A diamond is led to dummy's Queen. As East used a trump at trick 3, this draws the outstanding trumps.

Trick 9. A fourth round of clubs is trumped by South.

Now the last club in dummy is a master and dummy's King of spades is an entry. Thus declarer is able to dispose of (THROW OFF) his losing spade without risking a spade finesse.

57

Trumping in dummy

On many hands declarer postpones the drawing of trumps until some losing cards have been trumped, generally in the dummy. Here is a typical part score battle:

```
                    North
                    ♠ 6
                    ♡ Q J 6 3
                    ◇ K 10 6 4
     West           ♣ K 7 5 2        East
     ♠ A Q 9 7 3                     ♠ J 8 4 2
     ♡ 4                             ♡ 9 7 2
     ◇ Q 8 2                         ◇ A J 9 7
     ♣ J 9 8 3      South            ♣ Q 6
                    ♠ K 10 5
                    ♡ A K 10 8 5
                    ◇ 5 3
                    ♣ A 10 4
```

South deals and opens One Heart. The bidding goes:

South	West	North	East
1♡	1♠	2♡	2♠
pass	pass	3♡	pass
pass	pass		

West has no very obvious lead against Three Hearts. We will say that he chooses a low club.

Trick 1. West leads the 3 of clubs, dummy plays low, East plays the Queen and declarer the Ace.

South analyzes the play. He must expect the third round of clubs to be a loser, and if the Ace of diamonds is over the King he will have two losers in that suit. Thus he cannot afford to lose more than one spade. With the singleton in dummy this should not be difficult, but he must be careful to trump two spades before drawing all the trumps. The best play is a spade immediately.

Trick 2. South leads the 5 of spades and East wins with the 8.

Trick 3. East leads the 6 of clubs, the suit his partner led. South puts in the 10, West covers with the Jack, and North wins with the King.

Trick 4. A low heart is led to the King.

Trick 5. The 10 of spades is led and trumped by the Jack of hearts in dummy.

Trick 6. Declarer leads the 6 of hearts from dummy and wins with the Ace.

Trick 7. South's third spade is trumped by dummy's last heart.

South has made six tricks already and still has three good hearts left, so he is sure of the contract. If he had played even one round of trumps earlier he would have been in difficulties against best defense.

A cross-ruff

There are hands where declarer never draws trumps at all but seeks to make all his trumps separately. Since another word for trumping is RUFFING, this type of play is known as a CROSS-RUFF.

North
♠ 4
♡ A 10 3
♢ A J 6 5 3
♣ 8 7 4 2

West
♠ K Q 10 8
♡ 7 2
♢ Q 10 8
♣ K 10 6 5

East
♠ J 7 5 2
♡ 9 5 4
♢ K 9 7 2
♣ A Q

South
♠ A 9 6 3
♡ K Q J 8 6
♢ 4
♣ J 9 3

South has a minimum One Heart opening, justified because

he holds the major suits and fair distribution. The bidding:

South	West	North	East
1♡	pass	2♢	pass
2♡	pass	4♡	pass
pass	pass		

An opening trump lead, or two club leads followed by a switch to trumps, would beat this contract, but West's natural lead is the King of spades.

The two singletons point to a cross-ruff game. South aims to make five trumps in his own hand, three in dummy and two outside Aces.

Trick 1. South wins with Ace of spades.

Trick 2. A diamond is led to the Ace.

Trick 3. A diamond is trumped with the 6 of hearts.

Trick 4. A low spade is trumped with dummy's 3 of hearts.

Trick 5. A diamond, led from dummy, is trumped by the 8 of hearts.

Note that this play is not entirely safe, for West might be able to over-ruff. However, it would be premature for declarer to ruff high. Sooner or later South wants to make a trick with the 8, and the sooner he plays it the less likely that West will be out of diamonds and able to over-ruff.

When the 8 of hearts wins the trick (West having to follow to the third diamond), the contract is certain. South has made the first five tricks and still has A 10 of hearts in dummy, K Q J in his own hand. Nothing can prevent him from making these five tricks separately by continuing the cross-ruff.

8. The Opener's First Rebid

After the interval for play we return to the opener's bid on the second round of the auction. This will complete the groundwork for bidding. If the opening bid, the first response and the first rebid are well founded, you can't go far wrong at this game.

The rebid depends, naturally, on what partner's response has been. Broadly speaking, responses can be of three kinds—strong (such as Two No Trump or a double raise), limited (One No Trump or a single raise), and variable (a change of suit). Your rebid is simplest after one of the strong responses, so we will take these first.

Rebids after a strong response

After a response of 2NT

The response of Two No Trump indicates balanced distribution and 13 to 14 points. That will be enough for game even if yours was a weak opening bid. Your hand is:

(1) ♠ K 10 6
♡ J 4
◇ A Q 8 5
♣ K 7 4 2

A minimum 13 points, but after your One Diamond—Two No Trump you can go to game in Three No Trump. There will be at least 26 points in the combined hands.

When you hold a five-card major suit and a singleton you may repeat your major suit:

(2) ♠ K 8 5 3
♡ K Q 10 6 4
◊ 5
♣ A J 8

You rebid Three Hearts, suggesting that from your angle, game in the suit may be safer than in Three No Trump. If partner persists with Three No Trump, however, let it stand.

It is a bad habit to rebid a suit just because it contains five cards:

(3) ♠ A Q 8 6 4
♡ Q 5 3
◊ 6 4
♣ A Q 8

After One Spade—Two No Trump you need look no further than Three No Trump. A rebid of Three Spades would invite partner to bid the game in spades, and you have no reason to think that ten tricks in spades will be easier than nine at No Trump.

Even with a two-suited hand, Three No Trump may be the best contract:

(4) ♠ K 4   (5) ♠ Q 4
♡ A Q 9 6 3   ♡ K Q 6 4 2
◊ K J 8 6 2   ◊ A J 6 3
♣ 3   ♣ J 9

After One Heart—Two No Trump, you can rebid Three Diamonds on hand (4), because Four Hearts and Five Diamonds are both possible contracts. Here again, if partner persists with Three No Trump, don't fight him. On hand (5) there is no point in showing the diamonds over Two No Trump. Your hand is entirely suitable for play in Three No Trump.

When you have opened a strong hand, there is no need to

jump. Once partner has responded Two No Trump, any continuation is forcing to game.

A different situation arises when partner has passed originally. Then the range of his Two No Trump response will be 11 to 12½ rather than 13 to 14. A simple rebid by the opener of his own suit will no longer be forcing:

(6) ♠ J 6
♡ K J 9 7 6 3
♢ A Q 2
♣ 3 2

You open One Heart in third position and partner responds Two No Trump, having passed originally. You rebid Three Hearts, which he can pass. It follows that with a stronger opening you must jump to game or bid another suit.

After a double raise

After a raise to Three in a major you simply bid game in the suit, unless you have slam hopes:

(7) ♠ K 10 7 4 2
♡ Q 10
♢ A K 6 3
♣ 4 3

With a hand like this, after One Spade—Three Spades bid Four Spades, not Four Diamonds, which would be a slam suggestion.

After a double raise in a minor suit, you may bid a second suit to see if this will enable partner to bid Three No Trump.

(8) ♠ 6 2
♡ A J 6 3
♢ K 5
♣ K Q 10 7 4

After One Club—Three Clubs, bid Three Hearts.

Quite often you will have to rebid Three No Trump yourself even though you do not control all the other suits:

(9) ♠ 7 3 2
♡ A 4
◇ K J 10 6 5
♣ K Q 2

After One Diamond—Three Diamonds, bid Three No Trump and take your chance that the opponents will not lead, or cannot run, the spades.

After a jump in a new suit

When partner has made a forcing response, the general rule is to make natural rebids, except that there is no need to jump.

(10) ♠ K 10 6 2
♡ 6
◇ A Q 8 5 2
♣ A 5 4

You open One Diamond and partner responds Two Spades, indicating a holding of about 18 points. You will surely finish in a slam, as you have a FIT in spades and excellent controls, but for the moment a bid of Three Spades, confirming the suit, is your best move. If, after One Diamond, partner responds Two Hearts, let the bidding develop naturally with Two Spades. After One Diamond—Three Clubs, Three Diamonds is best for the moment. This keeps the bidding low, and you will learn more about partner's intentions from his next call.

Rebids after a limited response

After a response of 1NT

When partner responds One No Trump to your opening bid you know he has 6 to 9 points. In calculating your rebids, place him with an average 7 to 8. In general, you need a total of about 25 together to try for game at No Trump on a balanced hand.

(11) ♠ A J 6 5 2
♡ 7 3
◇ A Q 4
♣ K J 6

This sort of hand contains one of the game's biggest traps for an inexperienced player. It seems strong, and many a player will go to Three Spades or Three No Trump. But look at it this way: partner has about 7 or 8, you have 15 with no useful intermediates. That gives you a probable maximum of 23. Game in No Trump (25) will be uphill work at best, and game in a suit quite impossible. In the long run it will pay you handsomely to pass One No Trump.

You can raise to Two No Trump on 17 or 18, to Three No Trump on 19. Suit lengths and good intermediates make a difference, as always.

(12) ♠ 7 4
♡ A 8 5
◇ A K 10 7 4 2
♣ A 4

After One Diamond—One No Trump, anything less than Three No Trump would be cowardly, as you have eight likely tricks (although only 15 points) in your own hand. Never let the point count be your master.

When your hand is unbalanced, containing a singleton or void, you will generally bid again after One No Trump. To try for game in your own suit you need to be about an Ace better than minimum.

(13) ♠ K Q 9 6 4 2
♡ A J 5
◇ A 3 2
♣ J

After One Spade—One No Trump, rebid Three Spades. This

is not completely forcing, and if partner responded with a minimum (6 points), he will pass.

With a fair two-suited hand, up to about 17 points, you show your second suit at minimum level:

(14) ♠ A Q 8 6 2
♡ 4
◇ A K J 6 3
♣ Q 4

After One Spade—One No Trump, Two Diamonds is sufficient. Partner can pass if he prefers diamonds. If you held the Ace of clubs instead of the Queen, however, you would jump to Three Diamonds, forcing to game despite partner's limited hand.

After a single raise

On a fairly balanced hand you need about 17 points to try for game after a single raise:

(15) ♠ 7 4
♡ A J 8
◇ K Q J 5
♣ A J 5 3

A raise in a minor suit is even more limited than in a major, so after One Diamond—Two Diamonds you should have no hesitation in passing.

With a five-card major suit and fair distribution you can try for game with about a King better than minimum:

(16) ♠ A Q 8 6 4
♡ 8
◇ A J 10 5
♣ K J 4

After One Spade—Two Spades your hand is worth a game try of Three Diamonds. This new suit after partner's raise is forcing on partner for one round. If weak, partner will bid simply Three Spades, which you will pass. If he is better than minimum, he will bid Four Spades or make some other constructive call, such as Three Hearts or Four Diamonds.

With a six-card suit you can apply the following test to decide whether you are close to game. Take a trump away and see if you would still have an opening bid:

(17) ♠ K 2
♡ A Q 8 6 4 2
♢ A J 10
♣ 8 3

You open One Heart and are raised to Two Hearts. With a heart less you would still have a sound opening, so you can try for game with Three Hearts.

Rebids after a response at the level of One

Partner's response of One in a suit has a wide range, from 5 to 16 points. Until he has evidence to the contrary, the opener must assume a rather weak hand opposite. He should consider his own hand from two angles, asking himself:

Have I much in reserve after my opening bid?

Have I extra values in support of my partner's suit?

The answers to these questions are not always the same. Suppose you open One Diamond on:

(18) ♠ A 10 7 4
♡ 3
♢ A K 8 5 2
♣ K 10 6

Now if partner responds One Heart you reflect that you have only 14 points and by no means a remarkable hand. For the moment you rebid simply One Spade. But suppose partner responds One Spade. Now besides a singleton and good controls, you have strong spade support and can raise to Three Spades.

Like responses, rebids can be classified as limited, variable, encouraging, game-going, and forcing. We look at these in turn.

Rebids that show a limited opening

You indicate that you have a comparatively weak hand by one of the following rebids:

A rebid of One No Trump, showing a moderate balanced hand of about 13 to 16 points.

A simple rebid of your own suit.

A single raise of partner's suit.

For example, you hold:

(19) ♠ Q 4
♡ Q 7 6 4
◇ K 10 3
♣ A K 6 3

You open One Club. Over a response of One Spade you rebid One No Trump. Over a response of One Heart, raise to Two Hearts. Over One Diamond, a rebid of One Heart would not be a mistake, but One No Trump gives the better picture, as you have honors in every suit and the heart suit is not long.

When there is a choice between rebidding your own suit and raising partner's suit, a sound principle is to give preference to the raise of partner's suit if it is a major:

(20) ♠ A 10 5
♡ 7 3
◇ A Q J 4 2
♣ K 6 5

You open One Diamond and partner responds One Spade. The diamonds are rebiddable, but a raise to Two Spades is more likely to lead the partnership into a major-suit game, usually easier to make than game in a minor. Over One Heart the best rebid is One No Trump, giving a picture of fair all-round values.

Simple changes of suit that can be weak or strong

When you have a second suit, you can bid it at minimum level on hands ranging from 13 to about 19 points:

(21) ♠ 6 2
♡ A K 7 3
◇ A J
♣ A Q J 4 3

You open One Club and partner responds One Diamond. You need bid no more than One Heart. Partner will bid again unless his first response was sub-minimum.

A bid of a second suit at the Two level has a similar range:

(22) ♠ 7   (23) ♠ 7 5
♡ A Q J 6 4   ♡ A Q 10 6 4
◇ A K Q 4   ◇ K Q 9 6 3
♣ Q J 2   ♣ 4

Hand (22) is maximum for the sequence One Heart—One Spade—Two Diamonds. You would, however, bid the same way with (23). Note that partner can give preference in your first suit without going higher than the Two level. Compare with hand (24) on page 70.

Encouraging rebids, strongly inviting game

With an Ace better than a minimum opening, or with strong support for partner's response, or a strong suit of your own, you may choose one of the following rebids:

A jump to Two No Trump, suggesting about 18 to 20 points. For example:

♠ A Q 5   ♡ J 6   ◇ A K 9 6 4   ♣ K Q 8

After One Diamond—One Heart, rebid Two No Trump.

A double raise (jump) of partner's suit. For example:

♠ 5   ♡ K 10 7 6   ◇ A J 9   ♣ A K 8 4 2

After One Club—One Heart, raise to Three Hearts.

A jump rebid of your own suit:

♠ J 5   ♡ A Q J 9 7 6   ◇ A Q 3   ♣ K 4

After One Heart—One Spade, jump to Three Hearts.

Also encouraging is a sequence such as One Diamond—One

Spade—Two Hearts, where the second suit is higher in rank than the first and is bid at the Two level. This is called a RE-VERSE BID:

(24) ♠ 10 2
♡ A K 8 6
◇ A Q J 4 3
♣ K 5

You open One Diamond and, over One Spade or Two Clubs, you reverse with Two Hearts. The reason why you need to be strong to follow this sequence is that if partner is weak and wants to give preference to the first suit, diamonds, he must bid at the Three level.

Game bids

The three rebids in this category are Three No Trump, a raise to game in partner's suit, and a jump to game in your own suit. In each case the values are slightly greater than for the bids just short of game. A rebid of Three No Trump shows a hand in the 20 to 22 range. Here is an example of a raise to game in partner's suit:

(25) ♠ A Q J 4
♡ 3
◇ A K 8 5 2
♣ K 10 4

This is similar to hand (18), but with better spades. After One Diamond —One Spade you jump to Four Spades.

Forcing rebids

As always, the strongest bid is a jump in a new suit, forcing to game. This will often be based to some extent on a fit for partner's suit:

(26) ♠ 4
♡ K 10 4
◇ A K Q 8 5
♣ A K 6 2

After One Diamond—One Spade you bid simply Two Clubs,

because the hands may not fit well. After One Diamond—One
Heart, however, you force to game with Three Clubs, as game
in some denomination looks certain.

With very strong support for partner's suit you may have to
bid a non-existent suit in order to express your full strength:

(27) ♠ K Q 6 3
♡ —
♢ A K J 6 4 2
♣ A 10 3

After One Diamond—One Spade you are too strong to jump
to Four Spades. You can think of slam. For the moment you
force with Three Clubs. When you support spades later,
partner will realize that your force was based on spade strength.

Rebids after a response at the level of Two

When partner responds at the level of Two, you expect him
to hold upwards of 9 points (if less, he will hold a very strong
suit). The general pattern of rebids is mostly the same as over
a response of One.

The most limited rebid you can make is a repeat of your own
suit. This will generally suggest about 12 to 14 points, though
sometimes there will be no other choice on 15. After One
Heart—Two Clubs, or One Heart—Two Diamonds, rebid
Two Hearts on:

♠ K 10 5   ♡ A Q 10 8 7 4   ♢ K 5 2   ♣ 3

A new suit at a minimum level ranges from 12 to about 18:

(28) ♠ A 4
♡ A Q 8 6 4
♢ A K 8 5
♣ 5 4

You open One Heart and partner responds Two Clubs. There
will surely be a play for game at some denomination, but you
need bid no more than Two Diamonds. As partner had enough
to respond at the Two level he will bid again after you change
the suit.

Two No Trump is not, as you might expect, a minimum rebid after a response at the Two level. It shows a hand of about 15 to 17 points.

(29) ♠ Q 4
♡ A Q 8 4
◇ K 10 8 5
♣ Q 6 2

After One Heart—Two Clubs, either Two No Trump or Three Clubs would suggest more than you hold. The best rebid is Two Diamonds. Suppose you are stronger:

(30) ♠ A Q 10 7 4
♡ K 7 4
◇ Q 3
♣ A J 5

Now, after One Spade—Two Diamonds, Two No Trump expresses the hand well.

With about a King better than minimum you can make one of the stronger rebids, such as a jump in your own suit:

(31) ♠ A K J 9 7 6
♡ K 4
◇ A 10 8
♣ J 5

Open One Spade and jump to Three Spades after any response at the Two level.

A reverse bid shows additional values beyond a minimum opening:

(32) ♠ A K 8 4
♡ K Q J 7 4
◇ Q 8 4
♣ 3

After One Heart—Two Diamonds, reverse with Two Spades. After One Heart—Two Clubs, Two Hearts would be a sounder rebid. (Alternatively, you could open with One Spade and bid hearts on the next round.)

9. Strong Opening Bids of More than One

Two types of hand call for an opening bid of more than One. Very strong hands can be opened with Two No Trump or Three No Trump or Two of a suit. Weak hands with a long (six-card) suit, but little defensive value, are opened with a bid of Three or more. We will look at the strong hands first.

Opening 2NT and responses

The range for an opening Two No Trump is from about 21 to 23, with all suits guarded. These are typical hands:

(1) ♠ A Q 8   (2) ♠ K 7
     ♡ K J 10 4   ♡ A Q 10
     ◇ A K 5   ◇ A K J 10 5
     ♣ A J 9   ♣ K J 9

Responder can usually raise to Three No Trump on 4 points (a minimum 21 plus 4 equalling 25) or on a five-card suit headed by the King or on a six-card suit headed by a Jack. Any suit response at the level of Three is forcing:

(3) ♠ 10 7 3   (4) ♠ 10 4
     ♡ J 9 8 6 4   ♡ J 6 2
     ◇ 4   ◇ J 9 7 5 3 2
     ♣ Q 8 6 3   ♣ 7 6

On hand (3) respond Three Hearts. On hand (4) raise to Three No Trump. Partner will make this if he can bring in the long diamond suit, but there is little chance of Five Diamonds.

Opening 3NT and responses

An opening Three No Trump suggests either:

(*a*) An all-round hand containing 25 points, such as:

(5) ♠ K Q 6
♡ A Q J
◇ A K J 7
♣ A Q 10

or (*b*) A hand containing a strong minor suit, with the other suits guarded, such as:

(6) ♠ A Q
♡ K 10 4
◇ A K Q 10 8 4
♣ A 8

An advantage of opening Three No Trump on hand (6) is that the opening lead will come up to the big hand.

An opening Three No Trump should not be RESCUED by a responder who holds a long, weak suit:

(7) ♠ 10 8 6 5 3 2
♡ 6 3
◇ 9 5
♣ J 6 3

Pass an opening Three No Trump. Partner may have game in his own hand. It follows that any TAKEOUT of Three No Trump is an encouragement to slam.

The forcing Two

When you want to wave the big stick, you open with a bid of Two in a suit. This is forcing to game, and has been called a DEMAND BID. Partner is not allowed to pass short of game, however weak he may be.

The point count is *not* a very reliable guide for Two bids.

In terms of points the minimum is about 19 with very strong distribution, but what really matters is that you should have almost a sure game in your own hand:

$$(8) \quad \spadesuit \text{ A Q J 9 7 4}$$
$$\heartsuit \text{ A K Q 10 3}$$
$$\diamondsuit \text{ K 6}$$
$$\clubsuit \text{ —}$$

You are prepared to play in game even if partner has very little, for you can reasonably expect to win five spade and five heart tricks in your own hand. You intend to show both your suits, and you open Two Spades, the longer suit.

$$(9) \quad \spadesuit \text{ A K 4}$$
$$\heartsuit \text{ 5 3}$$
$$\diamondsuit \text{ A Q 8 7 4}$$
$$\clubsuit \text{ A K Q}$$

This is a much stronger hand in terms of high cards, but you cannot say that you have game in your own hand. The weakness in hearts makes Two No Trump unsuitable (though not unthinkable). Best is to open One Diamond and hope that partner can respond. If he can bid One Heart, for example, or One No Trump, you will go straight to Three No Trump.

$$(10) \quad \spadesuit \text{ A K J 2}$$
$$\heartsuit \text{ A 4}$$
$$\diamondsuit \text{ A K Q 3}$$
$$\clubsuit \text{ A J 8}$$

The 26 points are enough for Three No Trump, and that call would not be a mistake. Rather better, however, is to open Two Spades and show the diamonds on the next round. If partner can support either of your suits, a slam will not be far away.

Responses to Two bids

The weakness response to an opening Two bid is Two No Trump. With less than about 6 points it should be your first response:

(11) ♠ 5
♡ J 8 6 4
◇ 10 8 6 3 2
♣ Q 5 2

Clearly you will respond Two No Trump to an opening Two Spades. If the opening is Two of any other suit, you still begin with Two No Trump and show support later.

Any response other than Two No Trump is a positive response and promises some values:

(12) ♠ K 9 7 5
♡ 4
◇ 6 5 3
♣ Q 8 5 4 2

Raise Two Spades to Three Spades, or Two Clubs to Three Clubs. Over Two Hearts or Two Diamonds, however, you should respond Two No Trump.

(13) ♠ A 10 9 6 3
♡ 4 2
◇ 6 3
♣ J 10 6 4

The fair five-card spade suit headed by an Ace justifies a response of Two Spades over Two of any other suit. Over Two Spades, respond Three Spades.

Respond Three No Trump if you hold about 10 or 11 points, with stoppers (controls) or partial stoppers in the other three suits:

(14) ♠ Q 10 8 4
♡ J 5
◇ K J 6
♣ K J 4 2

Respond Three No Trump to Two Hearts. If partner opens
with Two Spades or Two Clubs, this would be a distinctly
useful hand, and you would give a single raise, setting the suit.
This single raise is a positive response and is enough on even
better hands than this.

A double raise promises good trump support, but in general
a rather weak hand for slam purposes:

(15) ♠ 8 4
♡ Q 10 8 6 2
◇ K 6 5 3
♣ 4 2

Raise Two Hearts to Four Hearts. You tell partner that you
have good hearts but little else—certainly not an Ace in a SIDE
SUIT.

A player who has responded negatively to an opening Two
bid has already limited his strength and must not be shy about
indicating quite modest values on the next round:

(16) ♠ 7 3
♡ Q 8 6 4 2
◇ 6 5
♣ 10 7 4 2

You respond Two No Trump to Two Spades and partner
follows with Three Diamonds. Remember that you have to
keep the bidding open until game is reached, so your choice
lies between Three Spades, Three Hearts, and Three No Trump.
Don't have any hesitation in showing your hearts. Partner has
opened with a Two bid because he wants to hear about such
small jewels as you may possess. Don't keep them hidden under
the table!

10. Pre-Emptive Openings of Three and Four

Opening bids of Three and Four are very different from the forcing Two. They are made on hands that are weak in high cards but contain a long suit, generally of seven cards or more.

Bids of this sort are known as PRE-EMPTIVE, a word that means *buy before*. You attempt to buy the contract before the opponents have begun to exchange information. You don't expect to make your contract, but the points you lose will be fewer than if you allow your opponents a free run to game. If they enter at this high level they may pick the wrong suit or run into your partner's strength. Suppose that as dealer you hold:

(1) ♠ K Q J 10 7 5 3
    ♡ 4
    ◇ J 10 5 2
    ♣ 7

This hand is too weak in high cards for an opening bid of One Spade, but you have just the right sort of hand for Three Spades. You cannot go far wrong in this contract, for you are almost sure to make six tricks in the trump suit alone. If partner has no tricks for you, then surely the opponents will hold practically all the high cards, sufficient for game or even slam.

If your high cards justify a bid of One, then you are too strong for a bid of Three:

(2) ♠ K 6
♡ A Q J 9 8 7 4
◊ Q J 5
♣ 2

With a hand of this sort, position at the table is important. If your partner had passed, and you were third hand, you might well open Three Hearts. The "worst" that could happen is that you might miss a game if partner had a maximum pass and did not raise. First or second to speak, open One. Otherwise, in playing with you, your partner will never know what your hand is like when you open with a Three bid.

An opening of Four in a major is even more likely to SHUT OUT the opponents, but it is more likely to be doubled and must be based on stronger values:

(3) ♠ 6
♡ A K 10 8 7 6 4 2
◊ 3
♣ K 6 4

Open Four Hearts, as you have eight likely tricks in your own hand.

Pre-emptive bids in a minor follow the same principles. A bid of Three Clubs or Three Diamonds is not so effective as a bid of Three Spades, obviously, but odd things happen at the table when players refuse to be shut out.

With exceptional length in a minor suit you may pre-empt at a higher level:

(4) ♠ —
♡ 6
◊ A K J 9 8 7 5 3
♣ Q J 9 6

Bid Five Diamonds. Note that these high calls are always semi-defensive, not an invitation to slam.

Responding to bids of Three and Four

To try for game opposite a weak Three bid you need about 14 points including two Aces and a King. Aces are important because partner will usually hold one or more singletons. Thus Queens and Jacks will often pull no weight.

(5) ♠ 6 3
♡ K Q 5 2
♢ A J 8 6 4
♣ A 3

You can just about raise Three Spades to Four Spades. Opposite a Three bid, of course, you do not require normal trump support. If you have enough strength in side suits you can raise on a singleton trump.

(6) ♠ K J 4
♡ 5
♢ A K 8 7 4 2
♣ Q 8 6

Here you can raise Three Spades to Four Spades because your singleton heart may be useful. Three Hearts you should pass. It would be a mistake to introduce Four Diamonds on two counts: You have no reason to suppose that your diamonds are as good as your partner's hearts, and secondly, you would be encouraging the opener to bid again. In general, any response in a new suit over a pre-emptive opening should be a forward move, not a rescue operation.

To try for a slam opposite an opening Four bid you need about 17 points, made up mostly of Aces and Kings:

(7) ♠ A 10
♡ 7 5
♢ K Q J 8
♣ A K 9 6 2

Over Four Hearts don't rush into Six No Trump or anything of that sort. A slam try of Five Hearts is enough. Partner will place you with two Aces at least. Alternatively, you might use the Blackwood convention, described in chapter 16.

11. How to Score

Before we come to the chapters that deal with defensive and competitive bidding, we must learn more about the scoring.

A score-sheet for bridge has two columns and a heavy line across the middle. It looks like this:

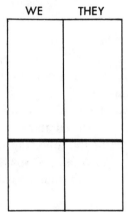

A player enters the score for his own side in the left-hand column, that of the opponents on the right. It is advisable for each player to keep his own tally as the score affects the bidding in many situations.

Scores below the line when the contract is made

(a) Not doubled

When the contract is for a part score (value less than 100), you write the total for tricks bid and made below the line, and any overtricks made but not bid, above. Suppose that the contract is Two Hearts and that nine tricks are made. You enter 60 below the line, and 30 above the line for the overtrick. Only the 60 counts toward game.

When the successful contract is for game, it is usual to enter the whole score below the line. Suppose that Three No Trump is bid and five made. Technically, this should be entered as 100 below and 60 above, but since it concludes a game, it makes no difference and it is shorter to write 160 below. When game has been made, a line is drawn beneath it, and the side is said to be VULNERABLE. From then on bonuses and penalties are increased.

(b) Doubled or redoubled

The trick score is multiplied by two when doubled, by four when redoubled. Thus Two No Trump doubled is worth 140 below the line and wins game.

Whenever a doubled or redoubled contract is made, declarer earns a fixed bonus of 50, scored above the line.

Overtricks are scored at the following rate: Not vulnerable, 100 for each doubled overtrick, 200 for each redoubled overtrick; vulnerable, 200 for each doubled overtrick, 400 for each redoubled overtrick.

Scores above the line

Slam bonuses

The bonus for grand slam (13 tricks) not vulnerable is 1,000; vulnerable, 1,500.

The bonus for small slam (12 tricks) not vulnerable is 500; vulnerable, 750.

Game and rubber points

No separate bonus is scored for a side's first game. The side that first wins two games out of three wins the rubber and scores points as follows: A bonus of 700 if the rubber has been won in two games, or 500 if the opponents have made a game.

Honors

The bonus for honors is scored whether the contract is made or not. Any player (whether declarer, dummy or defender) who holds in his own hand four honors in the trump suit scores a bonus of 100 for his team. If he holds all five honors the bonus is 150. In a No Trump contract all four Aces in one hand score 150.

Penalties for contract defeated

Now we look at the other side of the coin—the penalties for not making a contract. Penalties are scored above the line, and vary according to vulnerability. They go, of course, to the defenders for defeating the contract.

(a) *Not vulnerable*

Undoubled—50 for each undertrick.

Doubled—100 for the first undertrick, 200 for each subsequent undertrick.

Redoubled—200 for the first undertrick, 400 for each subsequent undertrick.

(b) *Vulnerable*

Undoubled—100 for each undertrick.

Doubled—200 for the first undertrick, 300 for each subsequent undertrick.

Redoubled—400 for the first undertrick, 600 for each subsequent undertrick.

A specimen rubber

At first glance scoring may seem more complicated than it really is. The same scores constantly recur and you soon know what they are without computing, just as you know what lunch has cost if you order many of the same items every day. It is only when some relatively uncommon event like Six No Trump doubled, vulnerable, with an overtrick occurs that you have to do some actual counting.

To be sure that you understand the method, you may like to prepare a score-sheet and write down the scores of a specimen rubber:

(1) You play Two Clubs and make four.

(2) You play Three Hearts doubled and go two down.

(3) Opponents bid One No Trump and make three. One of them holds four Aces.

(4) You bid Six No Trump and make it. (Remember to draw a line below to indicate a completed game.)

(5) Opponents play in Two Diamonds doubled and make two overtricks.

(6) You play Four Hearts doubled (vulnerable now) and go two down.

(7) Opponents bid Seven Diamonds and make it.

(8) Opponents play Three No Trump redoubled (they are vulnerable now too) and go one down.

(9) You play One No Trump doubled and just make it.

(10) You bid Six Clubs and make seven.

If you have kept the score accurately, it should look like the score-sheet on the opposite page.

The numbers in brackets refer to the deal on which the score was recorded. In some cases, scores for different items have been written in a single figure. For example, on hand 5 the bonus of 50 for doubled contract made and 200 for overtricks have been entered together as 250. The result of this adventurous rubber is that your side finishes 170 points ahead.

For the sake of completeness it should be added that if you must stop playing before a rubber is finished, a bonus of 300 is scored by the side that is a game ahead. If either side has a part score in an uncompleted game, a bonus of 50 is added.

A summary of the scoring table appears on page 150.

WE		THEY	
500	(10)	1000	(7)
750	(10)	500	(6)
50	(9)	250	(5)
400	(8)	150	(3)
500	(4)	60	(3)
40	(1)	300	(2)
40	(1)	40	(3)
190	(4)		
		80	(5)
		140	(7)
80	(9)		
140	(10)		
2690		2520	

12. Defensive Overcalls

When one side has opened the bidding, the first bid by a defender is called an OVERCALL or DEFENSIVE OVERCALL.

The defenders, in general, approach the bidding rather differently from the side that has opened. The opener and his partner are usually trying to go somewhere; usually, the defenders are trying to stop them. They are like irregular troops attempting to harass the enemy. Just as irregular troops have no great regard for appearance or discipline, so the defenders do not count their points or aim to bid accurately. They want to do as much damage as they can within a reasonable margin of safety.

Suppose that a vulnerable opponent on your right opens One Club. Not vulnerable, you hold:

(1) ♠ K Q 9 6 4 2
   ♡ 5 2
   ◇ J 7 4 3
   ♣ 6

An overcall of One Spade can achieve a number of aims:

Partner may have support for spades, and perhaps your side can go to Four Spades over, say, Four Hearts by the opponents. If you are doubled and go down two, losing 300, you will have made a profitable sacrifice against the vulnerable game.

The spade call will indicate a good lead to your partner, should the opponent on your left become declarer.

You may frighten opponents away from a Three No Trump contract.

A less obvious, but important, advantage of the overcall is that you take away some BIDDING SPACE from the opponents. The player on your left can no longer make a simple response of One Heart or One Diamond to the One Club opening.

A further point is that if you are doubled at a low level, such as in One Spade or Two Spades, and lose 500 points, in a sense that will not be costly. If you had not bid, then surely the opponents would have scored a vulnerable game. Your hand is clearly not strong in defense.

Here, by contrast, is the wrong sort of hand for an overcall:

(2) ♠ K Q 6
♡ Q 10 6 2
♢ 4
♣ A J 8 6 3

You are vulnerable and the bidding is opened on your right with One Heart. Now you have essentially a defensive hand if hearts become trump. To overcall now would be like emerging from a well-protected fort to engage superior numbers in open field. An overcall of Two Clubs could achieve little and might easily cost you 800 or even 1,100 points. You may not even have the consolation that you have saved a game, for your opponents probably cannot make a game against your holding.

So you see that high cards are not the test for a defensive overcall. Strength in your suit, vulnerability, and the level of the bidding are all important considerations. A good test is to assume that your partner has little or no support. If you can expect to make four tricks in your own hand you can overcall at the level of One, not vulnerable. Vulnerable, you should be able to make five tricks in your own hand.

To overcall at the level of Two you need a good suit and a

reasonable assurance that you will make five or six tricks even if partner is weak:

	(3)	♠ A 10 5		(4)	♠ J 6
		♡ J 6 4			♡ K 6 5
		◇ 9 5 3			◇ A Q J 8 5
		♣ A K 10 6			♣ 10 6 2

Hand (3) is altogether the wrong type for an overcall at the Two level. You are much too weak in playing strength and might make only three tricks playing in clubs. Hand (4) would be on the borderline for an overcall of Two Diamonds, not vulnerable. Vulnerable, it would be too risky in proportion to what it stands to gain. If the player on your left should hold ◇ K 10 x x, and a fair hand, he might double you and collect substantial penalties.

Jump overcalls

A jump overcall, such as Two Spades over One Diamond, or Three Clubs over One Heart, is a purely defensive call. It shows a strong suit but only about 7 to 10 points:

	(5)	♠ A Q J 9 7 6
		♡ 5 2
		◇ Q 6 4 3
		♣ 3

You can bid Two Spades over any suit opening on your right.

Overcall of 1NT

Sometimes, of course, the defenders will be strong enough to launch a counter-attack. With a balanced hand, One No Trump is the natural choice.

An overcall of One No Trump shows in principle the same sort of values as an opening bid of One No Trump. Naturally there must be a guard in the suit the opponent called. The player on your right opens One Heart and you hold:

(6) ♠ K 10
    ♡ A J 9
    ◇ Q 10 8
    ♣ K Q J 9 7

With a DOUBLE STOP (two stoppers) in hearts and a promising five-card suit, One No Trump expresses the hand better than an overcall of Two Clubs.

After the same bidding you hold:

(7) ♠ A 8
    ♡ K J 10 7 4
    ◇ K 8 4 2
    ♣ A Q

Now you have exceptionally strong defense against One Heart, and the best manoeuvre is a TRAP PASS, especially if opponents are vulnerable. As a general rule, if an opponent takes your opening bid away from you, the best answer—at least for the moment—is to pass. With no warning that the cards are stacked against them, the opponents may bid on to a higher contract, which you will be happy to double for worthwhile penalties.

Forcing overcalls

The strongest overcall you can make is a bid of the suit that an opponent has bid against you. (This is known as a CUE BID.) The opponent on your right opens One Heart and you hold:

(8) ♠ K Q J 7
    ♡ —
    ◇ A K J 7 3
    ♣ A Q 10 6

To express your very powerful hand you overcall with Two Hearts. In response, partner will bid his best suit, or will bid No Trump if his only length is in hearts. Your overcall in the opponent's suit is forcing for at least two rounds.

You may wonder what you are to do if an opponent opens One Heart and, sitting over him, you hold:

(9) ♠ A 6 3
♡ A Q 10 8 6 3
♢ J 10 4
♣ 5

Clearly you must not bid Two Hearts, for that, as we have just seen, would have quite a different meaning. Your best action for the moment is the trap pass. You hope that if One Heart is also passed by the responder, your partner in fourth position will be able to reopen the bidding.

13. Takeout Doubles

One very useful call is available to the defense that is quite different from anything we have met so far. Say that the bidding is opened on your right with One Diamond and you hold:

(1) ♠ K 10 7 4
♡ Q J 9 3
♦ 4
♣ A K 7 3

You would like to compete in one of your three suits. How can you find out which of the unbid suits is best for partner? Instead of guessing, you DOUBLE! That is an artificial call, for the natural meaning of the double is that you expect to beat the contract. This double at the level of One or Two, when partner has not made a positive bid, conveys the message: "I have a useful hand for offense—equal to an opening bid. Tell me where your strength lies." *Note that the double bears this meaning only when partner has not already named a suit.*

A takeout double is the right action on almost any hand that is too good for a simple overcall or has too many high cards for a jump overcall. The player on your right has opened One Diamond and you hold:

(2) ♠ A 4
♡ A K 10 9 3
♦ K 4
♣ Q J 8 5

Your first move should be a takeout double. On the next round you will probably be able to bid your hearts, and partner will know that you have an all-round hand with a strong heart suit.

Responding to a double

The duty of the doubler's partner is to show his best suit. Oddly enough, the weaker he is, the greater the obligation to bid *something*. Let us see why.

The bidding has gone:

South	West	North	East
1 ◇	double	pass	?

East holds:

(3) ♠ 9 6 3
♡ 7 5
◇ J 8 5 3
♣ 10 8 6 5

Not a pleasant situation, but the one thing East *must not do* is pass. He must bid Two Clubs—which promises absolutely no strength because it is forced. Defeat in Two Clubs will not be so costly as letting opponents make doubled overtricks in One Diamond. (The takeout double has the same effect on score as the penalty double.) If North makes an intervening bid, East is absolved from the necessity to bid with a bad hand.

When responder to the double has upwards of 7 points, plus a fair suit, he must jump to show that his hand is by no means worthless:

(4) ♠ K 10 8 6 3
♡ A 4
◇ 9 6 5 2
♣ J 7

This is a very fair hand in response to a double. It is worth a jump to Two Spades.

Still responding to the double of One Diamond, you hold:

(5) ♠ 5
♡ Q J 9 7 4 2
♢ 7 6 4
♣ A Q 5

Game in hearts is almost certain opposite a double. You can jump to Four Hearts.

When the defender's main strength is in the opponent's suit he will generally respond in No Trump:

(6A) ♠ 8 7	(6B) ♠ K 6 4
♡ Q 6 3	♡ 10 5 3
♢ K J 9 2	♢ K Q 10
♣ 7 5 3 2	♣ K 9 6 3

On hand (6A) respond to the double with One No Trump, and on (6B) with Two No Trump.

The only time when the responder to the double can think of passing is when he is exceptionally long and strong in the suit doubled:

(7) ♠ 7 2
♡ 6 3
♢ K Q 10 9 8 4
♣ 8 4 3

Now the best answer to partner's double of One Diamond is to pass. This, in effect, converts the takeout double into a penalty double. It also warns partner that you see no prospect of game in any of his suits.

Action by the opener's partner

After a takeout double by the defending side, what action should be taken by the partner of the opening bidder? The bidding begins:

South	West	North	East
1 ♡	double	?	

With a weak hand North can pass. With a fair to moderate

hand he makes his natural bid, such as One Spade or One No Trump or a raise of his partner's suit. With a good hand he redoubles:

(8) ♠ K 9 6 4
     ♡ 5 2
     ◇ A Q 3
     ♣ J 10 7 4

Holding 10 points, North can be sure that his side holds more than half the high card points. He redoubles, saying to his partner, "I think we've got them! Unless you are weak in defense we can double anything they say."

Doubling when two suits have been bid

The takeout double is a flexible weapon and can be used in many other situations. Here two suits have been bid:

South	West	North	East
1 ◇	pass	1 ♠	double

East's double suggests good support for both the unbid suits. He will hold something like:

(9) ♠ 4
     ♡ K Q 10 7
     ◇ A 8 6
     ♣ A J 9 6 4

Two doubles on the same hand

A player can double a second time after his first double has failed to extract a response. The bidding goes:

South	West	North	East
1 ♣	double	1 ◇	pass
pass	double		

Not content to let the opponents play in One Diamond, West doubles again to extract a bid from his partner.

Make sure that you perceive the difference between the last auction and one like this:

South	West	North	East
1♣	double	pass	1♡
2♣	double		

Here West's second double is for penalties, not for a takeout, because East has already shown his suit. It would be the same if East had bid One No Trump, or had doubled an intervention by North, or even had made a penalty pass, as in example (7) above. Let me repeat the basic principle: *A double is for a takeout at the range of One or Two only, and then only when partner has not already announced where his strength lies.*

Doubling after a pass

If you have passed originally you can double with less strength in high cards than when your hand has not been limited by the pass. The bidding goes:

South	West	North	East
pass	pass	pass	1♡
double			

South holds:

(10) ♠ Q 10 8 5
♡ 4
◇ K 10 3
♣ A 9 7 6 3

This would not be a sound double as second hand, but after your pass, it is the best way to counter-attack.

Double by the player who has opened

Use of the take-out double is not restricted to the defenders. The player who has opened can use the double to elicit a response from his partner. Take a sequence like this:

South	West	North	East
1♡	1♠	pass	pass

South has a strong hand, probably short in spades, and wants North to call his suit:

(11) ♠ 6
♡ A 10 7 4 3
◊ A K 8
♣ K Q 10 5

Overcalls in fourth position

So far we have been considering overcalls by the player sitting immediately over the adverse bid. Standards are rather different when the opening bid is followed by two passes.

South	*West*	*North*	*East*
1 ◊	pass	pass	?

East can REOPEN the bidding as it is called, on less than is required for an immediate overcall. Say that he holds:

(12) ♠ K 6 2
♡ A J 10 4
◊ 6 3
♣ J 6 4 2

It would be sissy for East to take the defeatist attitude, "They won't go far in One Diamond. Catch me reopening and giving them another chance!"

The odds are that East-West hold the better cards. North must be very weak to pass his partner's One Diamond, and West may be quite strong. East should contest the part score by reopening with One Heart. If he were a little stronger he would double.

Standards for One No Trump in this position are also a good deal lower than when sitting immediately over the bid:

(13) ♠ Q 8 4
♡ K 9 7 2
◇ A J 3
♣ Q 4 3

After an opening bid of One has been followed by two passes, you should reopen with One No Trump.

Defense against an opening 1NT

When an opponent has opened One No Trump, showing 16 to 18 points and some values in all the suits, it is particularly dangerous to intervene. The defender is in a very exposed position:

(14) ♠ K Q 9 6 3
♡ A K 4
◇ Q 7 5
♣ 6 2

On this sort of hand nothing is gained, and much is risked, by overcalling with Two Spades. Such an overcall should be made only with a much better suit, such as:

(15) ♠ K J 10 8 6 3 2
♡ A 8 6
◇ 5 3
♣ 2

There is no such thing as a takeout double of One No Trump. If a defender has the equivalent of a No Trump opening himself he can make a penalty double. His partner should leave this in unless he is weak and has a five-card suit. The bidding goes:

South	West	North	East
1NT	double	pass	?

East holds:

(16) ♠ J 6 4
♡ 10 7 5 2
◇ 9 5 3
♣ 8 6 4

East's best chance of escaping alive is to pass. Perhaps his partner has a good suit of his own and can lead it against One No Trump doubled. It will probably be easier to defeat One No Trump than to make Two Hearts, and even if the opponents make One No Trump doubled, they will not score a game.

Defense to Three bids

A double of an opening Three bid is primarily for a takeout. Suppose that an opponent opens with a pre-emptive Three Hearts and sitting over him you hold:

(17) ♠ K J 6 2
♡ 5 2
◇ A K J 4
♣ A 10 6

You can hardly risk Three Spades on such a moderate suit, and it would be cowardly to pass. The solution is to double. Partner will normally take out into his best suit, but if he has a balanced hand with at least one defensive trick in the trump suit, he may let the double stand for penalties.

14. Penalty Doubles

Let us be quite clear about the distinction between takeout doubles, as described in the last chapter, and penalty doubles.

If partner has made a bid of any kind, at any time, and in any denomination, then any double by you is a penalty double, made with the expectation of defeating the contract.

If partner has not spoken or has simply passed, then a double of One or Two of a suit is for a takeout. A double of an opening pre-emptive Three bid is primarily for takeout.

Doubling a low contract

You might think that the best penalty doubles would occur when opponents had contracted to make a large number of tricks. In fact, both the safest and most rewarding doubles tend to happen at a low level. You will seldom pick up 800 or more points from a freely bid contract at the game level or higher, but such penalties—worth much more than a game to your side—can often be extracted from a player who has made a rash or just an unlucky overcall at the range of One or Two.

Most opportunities occur when partner has opened the bidding and the next player has overcalled. Say that with both sides vulnerable the bidding goes:

South	West	North	East
1♡	2♣	?	—

Sitting North, you hold:

(1) ♠ Q 6 4 3 2
♡ 6
◇ A 8 5
♣ K 10 8 4

You have an excellent double, offering far better prospects

than Two Spades (which may hit a singleton in your partner's hand) or Two No Trump (which would be an unjustified overbid). You have two almost certain trump tricks in clubs, a possible trick in spades, a sure trick in diamonds, and a singleton in your partner's suit. This last factor is important, for it improves your prospects in defense. In addition, it suggests that you and your partner have a misfit. In that case it will pay you to defend rather than play the hand.

To decide whether you have a sound double, do not rely on points but try to estimate how many defensive tricks you hold. In the present example you have three sure tricks plus the Queen of spades. Your partner, who has opened the bidding, should be able to contribute at least three tricks in the play. If he has OPENED LIGHT—with a long suit and few high cards—he must take out the double into Two Hearts. So it looks as though you will take at least six tricks between you—enough to defeat Two Clubs. A further point is that Two Clubs doubled, if made because of freakish distribution, will not give the opponents game.

An intervention of One No Trump can often be effectively punished. With both sides vulnerable, your partner opens One Spade. Next player overcalls with One No Trump. You hold:

(2) ♠ J 4
♡ K 9 3
◇ Q 6 3
♣ K 10 7 4 2

You have a clear-cut double. Even if your partner has a minimum 12 or 13 points, your side will have the balance of the cards, with the advantage of the opening lead. The declarer will have a rough time, with probably a valueless dummy opposite him. Note that a double of One No Trump is more intelligent than overcalling with Two No Trump: if your side can make game in No Trump, taking nine tricks, then surely you will obtain a commensurate penalty by defending against One No Trump doubled.

100

Doubling a high contract

It will often happen, when the two sides are bidding competitively, that you will have a clear double of opponents who are SACRIFICING against your game contract. In general, if your partner has opened the bidding and you have a clear defensive trick such as an Ace, you can expect to defeat opponents who sacrifice against a game bid by your side.

It is important to realize, however, that the odds are loaded against a player who doubles a high contract. To take a common situation, suppose that non-vulnerable opponents bid freely to Four Spades. You hold:

(3) ♠ 7 4 3
♡ A K 10 5
♢ K Q 4
♣ Q 8 4

You have not entered the bidding and it will be your lead. You may think to yourself, "I have a couple of tricks in hearts, a likely trick in diamonds, and a possibility in clubs. My partner may contribute something as well. I am going to double Four Spades."

An opponent redoubles, your partner looks unhappy and passes. You pass and lead the King of hearts. Dummy goes down with a singleton heart, if not a void. They make an overtrick, scoring 480 below, 50 for making the contract, and 200 for the redoubled overtrick. Total 730, instead of an uneventful 150. Your double has cost 580. If you had got them one down (defeated their contract by one trick)—all you could reasonably hope—you would have scored 100 instead of 50.

Two reflections emerge from this sad tale. One is that the mathematics of the scoring table are against speculative doubles, the other that it is a bad mistake to double high suit contracts on the strength of Aces and Kings in the other suits. The more you hold in the side suits, the more likely that your opponents, who are not quite mad, will have distributional surprises for you.

The time to double, apart from occasions when opponents are obviously sacrificing, is when *you* have a surprise for *them*, particularly in the trump suit. If you have two *unexpected* trump tricks—a holding like J 10 9 x x—then probably you will defeat whatever contract is reached.

Penalty vs. game

Often you will have a choice between doubling opponents and bidding on to game. In general, it is right to accept a penalty of 300 or more when there is any doubt about the game for your side. When you are confident that you can make game, you should not be satisfied with a penalty of less than 500.

Looking at this matter from the other side, you do well to save a game at the cost of 300. If the penalty turns out to be 500, that is not, relatively speaking, a heavy loss.

15. Bidding from a Part Score

On many hands at rubber bridge one side or the other will have a part score below the line, and this will affect both the opening bid and the responses. If you have 60 below the line, for example, One No Trump will give you game, and you can make this bid on anything from 14 to 20 points. One No Trump is always a difficult bid for opponents to counter. They have to bid at the level of Two and are much exposed to a penalty double.

Opening with a part score

Opening suits bids of One are not much affected. It does not pay to make sub-minimum opening bids on the ground that there is not so far to go for game, for the opponents will surely contest. Nor is it necessary to go to the opposite extreme and be over-cautious.

The standards for opening Two bids are reduced when the bid is enough for game, but it remains a strong opening:

(1) ♠ A K J 9 6 3
♡ 5
♢ 6
♣ A Q 10 8 5

At 40 on score it is a sound tactic to open with Two Spades. If partner is very weak, he is free to use his judgment and pass.

Opening Three bids remain weak in principle, but again you can extend the range:

$$(2) \quad \spadesuit\ 5\ 3$$
$$\heartsuit\ A\ K\ Q\ 10\ 7\ 5$$
$$\diamondsuit\ K\ J\ 6\ 2$$
$$\clubsuit\ 4$$

If you had nothing on score this hand would be too strong for Three Hearts and you would open One Heart. With a part score of 40 you should open a strategic Three Hearts, even though this takes you one over game.

Responses with a part score

A sequence such as One Heart—Two Diamonds, which is forcing for one round when there is no score, is not forcing when Two Diamonds is enough for game. A jump to Three Diamonds would be forcing whether you had 40 or 90 points below the line. Partner must give you at least one more chance.

If you have 60 on score and your partner opens with a suit bid of One, you will naturally keep the bidding open if at all possible. A response of One No Trump would have a wide range, from about 3 to 13 points.

When opponents have a part score

In general, be aggressive when your opponents have a part score. Shade your One No Trump openings to 15 points. It is safer to open the bidding than to make a risky defensive bid when opponents have exchanged information and may be in a position to double for penalties.

16. The Way to Slam

It is exciting to bid and make a slam, but in the early stages you mustn't expect a high degree of accuracy. Slam bidding is an extension of earlier bidding, not (as some books appear to suggest) an art in itself. About one hand in ten, perhaps, is a makable slam, but the slam may not be biddable. *If you can bid half the slams that come your way, and fail only when unlucky, you will be doing better than most players.*

When to try for a slam

A small slam is worth bidding on just an even chance, such as a finesse for a King. To bid a grand slam, at the cost of losing a small slam, you need odds of at least 2 to 1 in your favor.

There are really two problems in slam bidding. The first is to judge when a slam may be possible, the second to approach it in the right way. Here are two tests that will help you, on many occasions, to judge whether you are in the slam zone:

1. If there are 33 points in the combined hands there will normally be a play for Six No Trump.

Partner opens One No Trump and you hold:

$$(1) \quad \spadesuit \text{ K J 4}$$
$$\heartsuit \text{ A 10 7 3}$$
$$\diamondsuit \text{ Q 4 2}$$
$$\clubsuit \text{ A Q 8}$$

You expect your partner to have 16 to 18 points, and you are contributing 16. Thus there is a minimum of 32 points in the combined hands, and a possibility of 34. Despite your flat distribution you can invite a slam by bidding Four No Trump.

In the next example your partner opens One Diamond and you hold:

(2) ♠ A Q J 6 3
♡ K Q 4
♢ Q 6
♣ A J 5

You force with Two Spades and partner rebids Two No Trump. That suggests a balanced hand, probably not less than 13 points. You have 19, a good five-card suit, and an honor in your partner's suit. There must surely be a play for Six No Trump.

2. If you could take an Ace away from your hand and still be confident of game, you can investigate a slam.

Partner opens One Spade and you hold:

(3) ♠ K 7
♡ A Q 10 6 4
♢ Q 3 2
♣ A J 5

You respond Two Hearts and partner raises to Four Hearts. Now if you had a small club instead of the Ace you would expect Four Hearts to be safe enough. So you are in the slam zone. The best approach is to show your Ace of clubs by bidding Five Clubs. When the trump suit (in this case, hearts) has been agreed by a double raise, a bid of a new suit shows a control, probably the Ace. This is called a cue bid because it shows a stopper, not a real suit. Your partner will go to Six Hearts unless he has two losers in the unbid suit, diamonds.

You open One Heart, holding:

(4) ♠ K Q 3
♡ K Q 8 5 2
♢ A K 5
♣ 6 4

Partner gives you a double raise to Three Hearts. Take away

your Ace of diamonds and you still have an opening bid. You can afford to make a slam suggestion below the game level. You cue-bid Four Diamonds, but if partner bids simply Four Hearts you give up.

Blackwood convention

Before you emerge from the chrysalis stage as a bridge player you will find that you are expected to know one or two conventions, among them the Blackwood convention. This is a method of showing a number of Aces in a single bid. Except in a sequence like One No Trump—Four No Trump, where no suit has been called, a bid of Four No Trump is CONVENTIONAL and asks partner how many Aces he holds. Partner responds according to the following pattern:

> With no Ace or four Aces.........Five Clubs
> With one Ace......................Five Diamonds
> With two Aces.....................Five Hearts
> With three Aces...................Five Spades

The player who has bid Four No Trump and has discovered that his side holds all the Aces may bid Five No Trump on the next round, to ask for Kings. Responses follow the same schedule—Six Clubs for no King, Six Diamonds for one King, and so on.

The time to use this convention is when your combined suits appear to be solid and you are interested only in particular Aces and Kings. For example, West and East hold:

West	East
♠ 10 4	♠ A K Q 9 6 3
♡ 6 3	♡ A K 5
◇ A K 8 6 5 2	◇ 7 3
♣ A J 4	♣ K 2

The bidding goes as follows:

West	East
1♦	2♠
3♦	3♠
4♠[1]	4NT[2]
5♡[3]	5NT[4]
6♦[5]	7♠[6]

[1]As partner has bid spades twice he must hold at least five and probably six. It is quite sound now to raise on a doubleton.

[2]Asking for Aces; Blackwood convention.

[3]Showing two Aces.

[4]All Aces accounted for, East is now asking for Kings.

[5]Showing one King.

[6]Barring an unexpected loser in spades, East can count twelve tricks on top—six spades, two hearts, two diamonds, and two clubs. There must be several possibilities of a thirteenth, such as a ruff in hearts in dummy, or the establishment of a long diamond.

Do not use Blackwood unless you can cope with any response that partner may make. Be especially careful when you intend to play in a minor suit. For example, suppose the agreed suit is clubs and you hope to make Six Clubs if partner has two Aces. Do not bid a Blackwood Four No Trump in this situation when you have only one Ace yourself, for if your partner has only one Ace, his response of Five Diamonds will carry you too high.

17. Defending Against No Trump Contracts

The play at no trump tends to develop into a race between the two sides to establish their long suits. Having the advantage of the opening lead, the defenders are first away in this race. For the most part they should back their best runner by leading their longest and strongest suit.

Opening leads

There are certain conventions in leading, based on practical considerations. We have mentioned already that when three honor cards are held in sequence it is usual to lead the highest. The most obvious reason for this is to avoid giving the declarer an easy trick. For example, a suit may be distributed in this way:

10 7

K Q J 8 6   5 4 2

A 9 5

It would not be clever for West to lead a low card and let dummy win a trick with the 10.

Another reason for leading a high card from a relatively short suit is to prepare an UNBLOCK:

K 7

Q J 10 5   9 8 6 4 2

A 3

As West, you can clear the suit in two rounds no matter which card you lead, but if you begin with the 5, instead of the Queen, you will block the run of the suit. You must retain the 5 to lead on the fourth round of the suit so that East can cash the fourth and fifth tricks.

It will be seen from the following table that the general rule is to lead the top of a sequence, or the higher of touching honors when one card is missing from a sequence. Thus the Queen is led from Q J 10 or Q J 9, but the 10 from Q 10 9. An exception to the general principle is that the King is led from A K Q or A K J.

From a suit of four cards or more headed by:

A K Q	lead	K
A K J	"	K
A Q J	"	Q
A J 10	"	J
K Q J	"	K
K Q 10	"	K
K J 10	"	J
Q J 10	"	Q
Q J 9	"	Q
J 10 9	"	J
J 10 8	"	J
A 10 9	"	10
K 10 9	"	10
Q 10 9	"	10
10 9 8	"	10

You also lead the 9 from a combination like 9 8 7 x, or the 8 from 8 7 6 x, partly to warn partner that you have no high honor, and partly to avoid a possible block on the fourth round. From other combinations, the standard lead is the fourth best—the fourth card from the top. The main object of this convention (you will remember these points better if you understand the reason for them) is to assist partner to judge, as the play develops, how many cards you hold in the suit you have led. Suppose that this is the distribution of the suit that has been led:

Q 8 4

A 10 5 3   J 7 2

K 9 6

West leads the 3, dummy plays the 4, East the Jack and South the King. East can tell at once that his partner has only four cards of the suit he has led. He knows this because the lead is the 3 and he holds the 2 himself. So partner cannot have a lower card than the 3. If that is the fourth best, he has only four cards. If he had five cards, he would have led the next-to-bottom. This knowledge may be very useful to East later in deciding whether to return his partner's suit or try something else.

In the same way, if the leader plays a low card and later plays one that is lower still, he is marked with a five-card suit at least:

A 6

Q 10 8 3 2   K 9 4

J 7 6

West leads the 3, dummy plays low, and the King wins. East

returns the 9 to dummy's Ace, and on this trick West plays the 2. East knows now that his partner started with five cards of the suit.

Here is another kind of inference that can be drawn from the lead of the fourth best:

J 8 3

A 9 6 5   K 10 7

Q 4 2

West leads the 5, dummy plays low, and East puts in the 10. This FINESSE AGAINST THE DUMMY is correct play, for West might have led away from the Queen. As it is, the 10 draws out South's Queen. East obtains the lead soon after in another suit. He cannot tell yet how many cards his partner has of the first suit, but he can be sure about the Ace. The 5 was led, and the only missing cards higher than the 5 are the A 9 6. His partner must hold them all if he has led his fourth best.

There is another way that leader's partner can arrive at the same conclusion—it is known as the RULE OF ELEVEN. You subtract from 11 the number of the card led, and the answer tells you how many cards higher than the one led are outside the leader's hand. Here you subtract 5 from 11. This tells you that six cards higher than the 5 are held by the players other than the leader. East can see five of those cards in his own hand and the dummy, so he knows that South has only one card higher than the 5.

Leading from a short suit

Quite often you may decide for a good reason not to lead your best suit. For one thing, it may have been bid by declarer or his partner. Alternatively, if you have a very poor hand, it may seem more sensible to play for possible tricks in your partner's hand. Say that you have to lead against Three No Trump from:

(1) ♠ 8 4 3
    ♡ J 8 6 2
    ◇ 7 3
    ♣ 10 7 5 3

Your best hope of beating the contract is to strike a long suit in your partner's hand. The exact bidding may provide a clue whether you should try spades or diamonds. If you choose a diamond, you lead the 7. Partner will generally be able to tell from the cards in sight that you have led from a short suit and not fourth best from a long suit. If you decide on a spade the 8 is the clearest card, though some players lead the middle card from three small cards and follow with the higher one next time the suit is played.

The lead when partner has bid

When your partner has bid a suit and opponents have reached a No Trump contract over it, you may have a delicate decision whether to lead his suit or your own. For example, your partner has bid diamonds and you have to lead against Three No Trump from:

(2) ♠ K 8 5
    ♡ Q 10 8 6 3
    ◇ 4
    ♣ 10 7 3 2

Should you be faithful to his suit or lead the 6 of hearts? The answer depends rather on the circumstances in which your partner has bid diamonds. If he has overcalled at the Two level, or at the One level when vulnerable, you must place him with a fair suit and should lead your singleton diamond. If he has opened the bidding with One Diamond then there is not the same assurance of a good suit, and you can reasonably try your own hearts.

However, when in doubt, you should lead your partner's suit. That is best for partnership morale. Few things are more annoying to a partner who has risked a weak bid in order to indicate a suit to lead than to see the opening leader go off on some wild goose chase of his own.

The next question is which card of partner's suit to lead. The general principle is to lead low from four cards or from three headed by a single honor, and to lead high from a doubleton or three small. From:

7 4	lead	7
7 4 2	"	7
7 5 4 2	"	2
Q 6	"	Q
Q J 6	"	Q
Q 10 6	"	6
J 7 3	"	3
Q 8 7 3	"	3

Why you lead a low card from three to an honor can be seen from this diagram:

8 5

Q 10 6   K 9 7 4 3

A J 2

If West begins with the Queen, declarer has a double stop. If he begins with the 6, then declarer's Jack can be trapped: the King will force out the Ace, and then West will have Q 10 over South's J 2. There are many such combinations where a trick is gained by keeping an honor over the declarer.

Ducking in defense

All the standard plays used by declarer are equally available to the defense. The mechanics of play are the same, after all, whoever plays the hand. In this example, a ducking play (see page 51) is employed by the defense.

```
                      North
                  ♠ Q 8 5 3
                  ♡ 10 5
                  ◇ K 9 2
                  ♣ K 9 7 2
        West                          East
     ♠ 10                          ♠ A 7 6 4 2
     ♡ K 8 7 4 3                   ♡ A 6 2
     ◇ 8 7 5                       ◇ Q 10 6
     ♣ J 10 6 4                    ♣ 5 3
                      South
                  ♠ K J 9
                  ♡ Q J 9
                  ◇ A J 4 3
                  ♣ A Q 8
```

South opens One No Trump, North raises to Two No Trump, and South bids the game.

Trick 1. West leads the 4 of hearts and East wins with the Ace. East will naturally return his partner's suit. With three cards, his right play is the next highest, the 6. With four cards, say the A 9 6 2, he would return the original fourth best, the 2. That is a very helpful arrangement in defense against No Trump contracts.

Trick 2. East leads the 6 of hearts. After South has played (either Queen or Jack), West sees that there is only one other card outstanding higher than the 6. He knows that if East held this card he would have returned it, so he reads East for A 6 2. (South would not have wasted the nine on trick 1 if he held the deuce.) Hoping that East will be on lead later to play his third heart, West ducks at this point, playing the 3. South holds the trick.

Tricks 3 to 5. South fears that if the opponents gain the lead they will defeat the contract by taking the Ace of spades and two more hearts. He hopes to make four tricks in clubs and four in diamonds if all goes well. So he plays off three top clubs, but is disappointed when, on the third round, East discards the 7 of

115

spades. (This unnecessarily high card is a signal which says that East has a controlling card in spades.) West now holds the high club, and the lead is ON THE TABLE (in dummy).

Trick 6. Declarer could attempt to win four tricks in diamonds now by finessing the Jack and then playing out the Ace and King, hoping for a 3 – 3 division. As that would give him only eight tricks, he tries first to steal a spade trick. He leads the 3 from dummy, but East is not asleep. He has noted his partner's play of the 4 of hearts, followed by the 3, and places him with a five-card heart suit. So he goes up with the Ace of spades.

Trick 7. East leads his third heart and West makes three heart tricks to defeat the contract.

I am sure you have not missed the main point—that if West had parted with the King of hearts at trick 2 he would never have enjoyed the long hearts.

Hold-up in defense

Our old friend, the hold-up, turns up this time on the other side of the table.

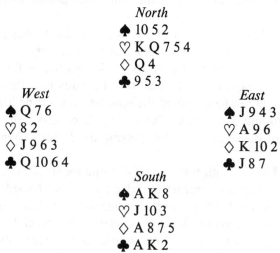

North
♠ 10 5 2
♡ K Q 7 5 4
◇ Q 4
♣ 9 5 3

West
♠ Q 7 6
♡ 8 2
◇ J 9 6 3
♣ Q 10 6 4

East
♠ J 9 4 3
♡ A 9 6
◇ K 10 2
♣ J 8 7

South
♠ A K 8
♡ J 10 3
◇ A 8 7 5
♣ A K 2

The bidding goes:

South	West	North	East
1 ◇¹	pass	1 ♡	pass
2NT	pass	3NT²	pass
pass	pass		

¹With three Aces and two Kings, South is a little too good for an opening One No Trump.

²North has little in reserve after his first response, but with a five-card suit and 7 well-placed points, he can expect a good play for game after his partner's strong rebid.

West leads the 4 of clubs and South wins with the King. He attacks hearts at once, and we do not need to follow the play trick by trick to see that the result depends on whether East releases his Ace of hearts too early. If East plays the Ace on the first or second round, South will make nine tricks easily. If East holds up until the third round, declarer will have no entry to dummy for the long hearts.

The "echo" at No Trump

You may ask, how did East in the previous hand know exactly how long to hold up his Ace? After all, if South had only two hearts it would be better for the defense to capture the second round, holding the declarer to only one trick in the suit. The answer lies in another form of defensive signal. When South leads the Jack of hearts at trick 2, West assumes that his partner, not South, has the Ace. (If South has the Ace too, he will run the hearts without difficulty.) To show partner that he holds a doubleton, West begins an ECHO, playing the 8 and following with the lower card on the next round. If West had three small cards he would play the lowest on the first round. At No Trump the echo to show a doubleton is used mostly when declarer is in process of establishing his own long suits. It gives a defending partner the count (by deduction) of *declarer's* holding, so he knows how long to hold up.

Unblocking in defense

All forms of unblocking are just as important for the defenders as for the declarer. Here are two typical situations:

♠ 7 4 3

♠ Q J 10 8 2   ♠ K 6

♠ A 9 5

Defending against a No Trump contract, West leads the Queen of spades. East must be careful to unblock by playing the King on this trick. If he fails to do so, South may take the Ace at once, leaving the suit blocked. More likely, South will duck on the first round and again on the second. Then, having won with the King, East will have no more spades to play, and West will need *two* entries to establish and run his suit.

Just as often, the defenders have to unblock with low cards:

♠ 7

♠ K J 8 5 3   ♠ A 9 6 4

♠ Q 10 2

Defending against Three No Trump, West leads the 5 and East wins with the Ace. East returns the 4, the original fourth best. West captures the 10 with the Jack and plays the King. Now East must take care to drop his 9. Otherwise he will be left in the lead on the next round, and West may have no entry to make the fifth spade.

18. Defending Against Suit Contracts

Opening leads against a suit contract do not follow the same pattern as against No Trump. There is normally no advantage in leading a long suit in order to establish low cards as winners. Even if this can be done, declarer will usually have enough trumps to ruff the later rounds.

Leading for safety

Against most contracts at the game level an important consideration is to make a lead that will not of itself give away a trick, such as the lead of a King up to declarer's A Q. The best lead is one that is both safe and constructive. In suits headed by A *K* Q, A *K* J, *K* Q J, *Q* J 10, or *J* 10 9, lead the italicized cards.

A long suit headed by A K is usually a good and safe lead. It enables you to see the dummy before leading to the second trick, and sometimes partner will play HIGH-LOW as a "come-on signal." Study these two situations:

(1)		J 10 4	(2)		J 10 4
A K 9 7 5	8 3		A K 9 7 5		Q 8 3
		Q 6 2			6 2

The King is led and in each case East signals with the 8. In example (1) he plans to ruff the third round. In (2) he signals because he knows that a continuation is safe. If declarer does not follow suit he will have to expend one of his valuable trumps to win the trick.

Against a No Trump contract you would lead a low card from A K x x x, retaining your high cards for entry, but that type of leisurely lead would be wasted against a suit bid. In the same way you lead the top card from K Q x x x or Q J x x against a suit contract, aiming at quick tricks. The lead from a suit headed by an unsupported Ace tends to give a trick away, but if you do lead that suit you start with the Ace.

Short suit leads

In order to avoid a lead that is obviously bad, you must often settle for one which is merely neutral, such as a lead from a short suit. Leading from 7 6 4, you can hardly give a trick away —at worst, you kill an honor in partner's hand that was probably dead anyway. A high-low lead from a doubleton has the added advantage that it may lead to a ruff for your side. A singleton lead has an even better chance: if you can find your partner with the Ace of your suit, you will get an immediate ruff. Also if partner holds a quick trick in the trump suit, he will be able to take the first trump trick and then give you a ruff in your blanked suit, before declarer exhausts your trumps.

Attacking leads

Quite often the opponents will have bid two or three suits and your choice of leads will be narrowed. What would normally be a dangerous lead from a holding like K J x or A Q x or Q x x or even K x can become your only choice.

This is a fascinating but not an easy subject. Understanding is more important than memorizing a table of preferred leads for every occasion. In the examples that follow, the lead is determined by tactical considerations based on the bidding and by the general make-up of the leader's hand.

120

Playing a forcing game

There is one special situation where the lead from a long suit is indicated. That is when you have length in the trump suit and hope to weaken the declarer's control by shortening his trumps. Here is an example:

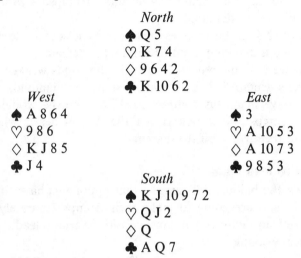

North
♠ Q 5
♡ K 7 4
◇ 9 6 4 2
♣ K 10 6 2

West
♠ A 8 6 4
♡ 9 8 6
◇ K J 8 5
♣ J 4

East
♠ 3
♡ A 10 5 3
◇ A 10 7 3
♣ 9 8 5 3

South
♠ K J 10 9 7 2
♡ Q J 2
◇ Q
♣ A Q 7

The bidding goes:

South	West	North	East
1♠	pass	1NT	pass
3♠	pass	4♠	pass
pass	pass		

The 9 of hearts would be a safe lead on West's hand, and another possible lead is the Jack of clubs. However, the strong holding in the trump suit points to an attacking lead from the leader's long suit. The advantage of this will quickly appear.

Trick 1. West leads ◇5 and East wins with the Ace.

Trick 2. East returns ◇3 and South ruffs.

Tricks 3 & 4. South leads a spade to the Queen and leads back dummy's last spade. East discards a heart, South plays the nine and West wins with the Ace.

121

Trick 5. West leads another diamond, forcing South to ruff again. Now that South has ruffed twice, he and West each have two trumps left.

Tricks 6 & 7. South draws the two remaining trumps.

Tricks 8 to 11. South cashes four tricks in clubs. East, meanwhile, knowing that South has no more trumps, is careful to retain his fourth diamond.

Tricks 12 & 13. East makes the last two tricks with the Ace of hearts and a diamond. South's contract is defeated.

You see how the repeated forces in diamonds weakened the declarer's trumps? Against any lead but a diamond, South would have made his contract easily because he would have drawn trumps and KNOCKED OUT the Ace of hearts while he still had trumps to ruff the diamonds.

When to lead trumps

Often the bidding will suggest that opponents have found a good fit and are going to make their trumps separately by a cross-ruff. In that case you must consider a trump lead. Here is a typical example:

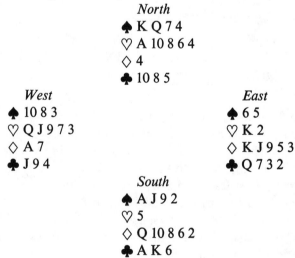

North
♠ K Q 7 4
♡ A 10 8 6 4
◇ 4
♣ 10 8 5

West
♠ 10 8 3
♡ Q J 9 7 3
◇ A 7
♣ J 9 4

East
♠ 6 5
♡ K 2
◇ K J 9 5 3
♣ Q 7 3 2

South
♠ A J 9 2
♡ 5
◇ Q 10 8 6 2
♣ A K 6

The bidding goes:

South	West	North	East
1 ◇	pass	1 ♡	pass
1 ♠	pass	3 ♠	pass
4 ♠	pass	pass	pass

The sudden acceleration of the bidding when spades are mentioned clearly suggests that the opponents plan to make tricks by ruffing. Moreover, from his shortage in diamonds and length in hearts, West judges that the declarer will have difficulty in establishing either of these side suits. West leads a trump, therefore, to reduce the ruffing power of declarer and dummy.

The trump turns out to be a killing lead. Imagine, first, that West makes some other lead, such as a low club. Declarer will win and play a diamond at once, preparing a cross-ruff. East wins and leads a trump—too late! South will play Ace of hearts and ruff a heart, cash the King of clubs, ruff a diamond, and so on, making altogether seven tricks in the trump suit and three top tricks in the side suits.

Now see the effect of a trump lead by West. South wins and gives up a diamond. The defenders lead a second round of trumps. Now South is one trick short. The most he can make in the trump suit is four tricks in his own hand, plus two by ruffing. Nothing can be done with the red suits, and South has to go down one.

19. Tricks in a Single Suit

Before you can plan, as declarer, the play of a complete hand, you must know how to handle various card combinations within a suit. Proper play enables you to take advantage of fortunate distribution. Remove 13 cards of one suit and lay them out according to the following diagrams. Then play them out to prove to yourself exactly why certain plays succeed while others fail.

Where a "finesse" is wrong play

Imagine that, playing the hand as South at No Trumps, you have this combination:

Q 7 2

A 8 4 3

You know you can make a trick with the Ace, but what about the Queen? Should you lead the Queen and finesse it? No. The best plan is to lead up to the Queen. That will gain when the King is on the left, as in this diagram:

Q 7 2

K 10 5   J 9 6

A 8 4 3

If the suit breaks 3 – 3, you can actually make three tricks, having lost one.

Perhaps you think that if the King were on the other side a "finesse" (not really a finesse because it is not promoting a lower card) would produce better results:

Q 7 2

J 10 5   K 9 6

A 8 4 3

Now if you lead the Queen from dummy, East will cover with the King, following the general rule in defense of covering a single honor with an honor. You can capture this trick with the Ace, but the defense will win the next two rounds.

This is a similar position:

J 5

A K 6 3 2

The best way to develop the most tricks (four) is to lead up to the Jack. That gains a trick (as compared with any other method) when the distribution is:

J 5

Q 10 8 4   9 7

A K 6 3 2

You lead the 2 toward dummy's J 5. If West goes up with the Queen, you make the Jack on the next round and the A K 6 as soon as you get back to your hand. Leading the Jack from dummy would not gain in any circumstances against correct defense. East, with Q x, or Q 10 x, or Q 10 x x, would cover the Jack with the Queen.

Even when you have the Ace, Queen and Jack in the two

hands a finesse may not be the best play. You will often have to tackle this situation:

Q J 6 4

A 7 2

Here, if the King is held by East, you can win two tricks without losing the lead by playing the Queen and finessing. Sometimes you will play the suit in that way, but if you are aiming to develop three tricks the best plan is to lead up to the Q J x x. That will gain a trick (as compared with leading the Queen) when the suit is distributed in either of these ways:

(1)   Q J 6 4

K 8   10 9 5 3

A 7 2

(2)   Q J 6 4

K 10 8 5   9 3

A 7 2

In both cases you win three tricks provided that you play toward, and not away from, the Q J.

Leading low for a finesse

In finessing, there is a general rule that unless you have a strong sequence you should begin with a low card. This is a frequent combination:

A Q 7 5 3

K 9   10 8 6

J 4 2

As the cards lie, you can make five tricks so long as you

begin with a low card from South towards the TENACE (highest and third highest cards) in dummy. You finesse the Queen and then lay down the Ace, on which the King falls. That leaves the Jack as master. You see what happens if you lead the Jack first? West covers with the King, and East's 10 is promoted to win the third round.

Here is one of many similar positions where it is easy to slip up:

A K 10 4

Q 8   9 6 5 3

J 7 2

The right technique is to lead low and finesse the 10. On the next round you lay down the King or Ace. As the cards lie, that wins four tricks. If you lead the Jack originally, or even on the second round, you lose a trick eventually to East's 9. It is the same with 10 x x opposite A Q J x: to lead the 10 costs a trick when the next player holds K x.

You can afford to lead a high card when you hold all the intermediate cards in sequence:

A J 10 4

K 8 5 2   7 3

Q 9 6

Now if the Queen or 9 is covered by the King, no card is promoted for the opponents and you still make four tricks. With this combination the 9 is the best lead, because it enables you to run all the tricks without needing a second entry to your hand.

Finessing against two cards

We look next at the way to play a number of combinations where two or more critical honors are missing. When declarer takes a finesse that will win if two cards are right for him he is said to take a DOUBLE FINESSE:

7 5 3

9 8 4   K J 6

A Q 10 2

Playing first from the North hand, you lead the 3. When East plays low you put in the 10. As the cards lie, this holds the trick. When next in dummy you lead for a finesse of the Queen and eventually make all four tricks. Had the 10 lost to the Jack on the first round you would have finessed the Queen later.

The following position is essentially the same:

K J 5

7 6 2

On the first round you finesse the Jack. If you are lucky enough to find West with Ace and Queen, you can make two tricks. If the adverse honors are divided, you still make one trick so long as you lead twice up to the K J x.

This is a slightly more complicated situation:

A Q 9 6 5

J 10 4   K 8

7 3 2

You lead the 2 and West plays low. Now if you finesse the Queen it will lose to the King and, after playing the Ace, you will have to give up another trick to West's J. The right play is to take a DEEP FINESSE of dummy's 9. As the cards lie, the 9 forces out the King. Note that it would make no difference if West were to SPLIT HIS HONORS by putting in the J or 10. In that case you would cover with the Queen and later finesse the 9. Nor can the deep finesse of the 9 on the first round cost a trick. Suppose the distribution to be:

A Q 9 6 5

K 10 4   J 8

7 3 2

Now it is true that you could finesse the Queen successfully on the first round, but you would still have to give up one trick. The effect is the same if you finesse the 9, losing to the Jack, and finesse the Queen next time.

Finesse or drop?

There are some situations where it is not immediately clear whether declarer should finesse or play out the top cards, hoping that the missing honor will fall. This is a combination that you will encounter many times:

K 8 2

A J 7 6 3

You lead the King and then small toward the A J 7 6. East follows suit, but the Queen does not appear. Now the odds slightly favor a finesse of the Jack rather than PLAYING FOR THE DROP by going up with the Ace.

There is an old saying, "Eight even, nine never," which bears on this position. With *eight* cards in the two hands, as in the example above, the finesse is right, but with *nine* cards you

have, in theory, a slightly better chance if you play the Ace
and King without finessing.

A 8 5 3

K J 7 4 2

You lead the Ace from dummy and then small toward
K J 7 4. If East follows on both occasions, and the Queen has
not appeared, the best chance, now that you hold nine cards in
the two hands, is to play the King, hoping to drop the Queen.

With ten cards, missing the King, the percentage play is to
finesse:

10 9 5 3

A Q J 8 6 4

You lead the 10 from North and East follows with the 7 or 2.
The best chance is to finesse. With eleven cards, missing K x
only, the odds favor playing for the drop of the King.

Safety plays

There is a large and important group of what are known as
SAFETY PLAYS. Here you have a perfect safety play in that you
can ensure against the loss of a trick however the cards lie:

A Q 10 8 4

K 9 6 3

You begin by leading low towards the Queen. Then if either
player SHOWS OUT, failing to follow suit, you can finesse against
his partner on the next round. If you make the mistake of
laying down the King first you have to lose a trick if West is
void and East holds J x x x.

Take away the 10 from the combination above, and you are
left with a *partial* safety play:

AQ842

K963

Now you should play the King first. In case East is void, this will enable you to pick up J 10 x x in West's hand. After the King you follow with the 3. West, with J 10 x now, must put in the 10, to prevent you from finessing the 8. You cover the 10 with the Queen and return to your hand to take another finesse through West's J x. If East has the four missing cards you must lose one trick however you play, so this is not a perfect safety play.

"How many tricks do I need?"

In the examples so far, we have been considering how to play various combinations without reference to the tactical situation. In actual play your handling of a particular suit will often depend on how many tricks you need from it. Often, like a man who pays a small premium as insurance against a major accident, you will give up a trick as a safety play to increase your chance of making the contract. Here is one of the most important plays in this group:

8642

AQ753

If you need all five tricks you finesse the Queen, hoping to find East with K x precisely, and J 10 in West's hand. Now suppose that you could afford to lose one trick, needing only four to be sure of your contract. The distribution might be:

8642

K   J 10 9

AQ753

The safety play is to begin by laying down the Ace. If the

King does not fall, you enter dummy and lead up to the Queen. You still make four tricks when East has K x or K x x.

The same safety play is right with this holding:

A Q 10 7 4 2

8 5 3

Needing five tricks, you lay down the Ace first, then return to your hand and lead up to the dummy. You will make five tricks except when East has K J x, and that you can do nothing about in any case. See what may happen if you finesse the Queen on the first round:

A Q 10 7 4 2

J 9 6   K

8 5 3

The Queen loses to the King. When next in your hand you lead the 5, on which West plays the 9. If you could see the cards you would finesse the 10, but that would be fatal should East hold K J alone. You have to guess on the second round, whereas by playing the Ace first you avoid any subsequent guess.

Finessing for safety

There are many positions where a finesse is taken to provide against a particular distribution. This is one of the more obvious examples, because the finesse cannot cost a trick—it can only save one:

K 8 3

9   Q J 7 4

A 10 6 5 2

You begin with the King from dummy and follow with the 3.

East plays low, for in most circumstances it could not help him to split his honors. Now you must lose one trick anyway, with the Queen and Jack still against you. To ensure against losing two tricks you put in the 10. Lay out the cards, dividing the adverse holdings in various ways, and see for yourself!

The same sort of play is indicated when you are missing K Q x:

10 6 4 2

A J 8 7 5 3

You lead the 2 from dummy and East plays the 9. As a precaution lest East hold K Q 9, you finesse the Jack—a play that cannot possibly cost a trick.

Sometimes, for complete safety, you will take a finesse that in all likelihood will cost you one trick. Here is a combination with startling possibilities:

K 9 6 4

A 10 8 5 2

If you aspire to make all the tricks you will naturally begin by playing the Ace or King. If an honor falls you may be left with a guess on the next round whether to play for the drop of Q J or to finesse.

But suppose you are in a small slam contract and that your only loser is in this suit. You will gladly give up *one* trick so long as you can be sure you don't lose *two* tricks. You lead the 2, West plays the 3, and you astonish your adversary by putting on the 4! This deep finesse (of course, the 6 or 9 would be equally effective) is a sure safety play to lose only one trick. The distribution may be:

                    K 9 6 4

    Q J 7 3   —

            A 10 8 5 2

You would also be safe if on your lead of the 2 West showed
out, marking East with Q J x x. To lay down the Ace or King
first, on the other hand, would be fatal if Q J x x were on the
wrong side.

There are numerous safety plays of this sort. You will find it
good practice, when you meet a new combination, to study it
(after the game!) in this light:

"How many tricks can I make at best?"

"Is there a safety play that will ensure my making all the
tricks?"

"Is there a play to ensure that I lose one trick at most? Or two
tricks?" And so on.

20. Finishing The Rubber

Let us now take up the play in an imaginary rubber where the players are up to all the tricks that have been described. Both sides are vulnerable, with no score below the line in the deciding game.

Trump control

South deals and distributes the cards as follows:

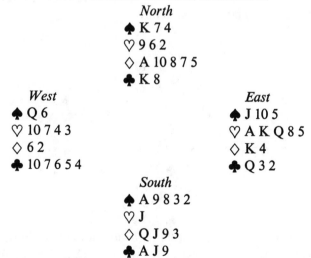

North
♠ K 7 4
♡ 9 6 2
♢ A 10 8 7 5
♣ K 8

West
♠ Q 6
♡ 10 7 4 3
♢ 6 2
♣ 10 7 6 5 4

East
♠ J 10 5
♡ A K Q 8 5
♢ K 4
♣ Q 3 2

South
♠ A 9 8 3 2
♡ J
♢ Q J 9 3
♣ A J 9

South opens One Spade and the bidding continues:

South	West	North	East
1♠	pass	2◇[1]	2♡
3◇	pass	3♠[2]	pass
4♠[3]	pass	pass	pass

[1]The spades are not good enough for an immediate double raise, so North bids Two Diamonds—a one-round force.

[2]This delayed support does not suggest such good trumps as an immediate raise.

[3]South has a minimum opening in terms of points, but he has a good fit for his partner's diamonds and a singleton in the right place, the opponent's suit.

Trick 1. West leads the 3 of hearts (his partner's suit), and East wins.

Trick 2. A second round of hearts is trumped by South.

Trick 3. Declarer must draw at least two rounds of trumps, as otherwise there may be a diamond ruff by the defenders. He leads the 3 of spades to dummy's King.

Trick 4. Declarer leads a second spade from dummy and wins with the Ace. The position is now:

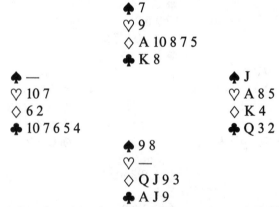

Knowing that there is still one trump out against him, South leads the 8 of spades. East wins with the Jack and plays another heart, which declarer has to ruff with his last spade.

South has lost two tricks already, and he still has to establish the diamonds. When East wins with the King of diamonds he makes two more hearts, defeating the contract by two tricks.

"I think I muddled that," says South. "Don't all speak at once!"

It is soon agreed that his mistake was in playing the third round of trumps. Look again at the last diagram position, and imagine that instead of playing a trump, declarer takes the diamond finesse and it loses. Now East can cash the Jack of spades and force declarer with another heart, but South makes the rest of the tricks without any difficulty.

The lesson that emerges is this:

Unless you have trumps to spare, don't lead an extra round to force out an opponent's master trump. Continue to develop your own side suits, and let your opponents make their trump in their own time.

Stayman convention for a part score

West deals as follows:

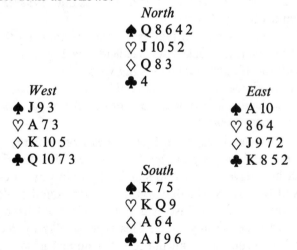

```
                North
                ♠ Q 8 6 4 2
                ♡ J 10 5 2
                ◇ Q 8 3
                ♣ 4
   West                          East
   ♠ J 9 3                       ♠ A 10
   ♡ A 7 3                       ♡ 8 6 4
   ◇ K 10 5                      ◇ J 9 7 2
   ♣ Q 10 7 3                    ♣ K 8 5 2
                South
                ♠ K 7 5
                ♡ K Q 9
                ◇ A 6 4
                ♣ A J 9 6
```

After three passes South opens One No Trump. His partner,

with no strength but with some length in the majors, uses the Stayman convention (see page 42) in search of a safe part score:

South	West	North	East
—	pass	pass	pass
1NT	pass	2♣	pass
2♢	pass	2♠	pass
pass	pass		

North hoped that his partner would be able to bid hearts or spades over the conventional Two Clubs. As Two Diamonds simply denied length in either major, North thought it advisable to transfer to Two Spades. With just an average No Trump, South had nothing more to say.

This time you have to visualize the hand being played by North, instead of by South, as in previous examples. With no clearly marked lead, East chooses the 2 of diamonds as his opening.

Trick 1. Dummy (South) plays low on the diamond lead and West wins with the King.

Trick 2. West returns the 10 of diamonds and declarer wins in his hand with the Queen.

Trick 3. North's natural play is to draw trumps, so that he can make some heart tricks later. He leads the 2 of spades, East plays with the 10, and dummy's King wins.

Declarer assumes now that East holds the Ace of spades, for if West had held it he would have captured the King. Note the play to the next trick:

Trick 4. Declarer leads the 5 of spades from dummy, West plays the 9, and North plays low! East's Ace wins the trick.

North has played the trump suit in the only way to escape the loss of two tricks. His duck on the second round could not be a losing play, for if East held A J 10 he would have been sure of two tricks in any event. This type of play by declarer (the duck to bring down an unprotected honor) is sometimes called an OBLIGATORY FINESSE.

We need not follow the rest of the play in detail. North can draw the outstanding trump with the Queen and force out the Ace of hearts. All he loses is one spade, one heart, and one diamond. He has made ten tricks, but the game was lucky and NOT BIDDABLE.

A sacrifice to save game

The next hand, dealt by North, contains several interesting points in competitive bidding.

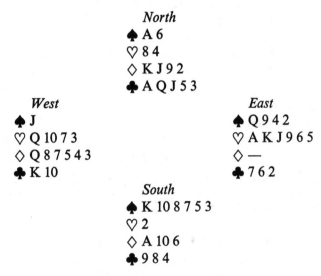

North
♠ A 6
♡ 8 4
♢ K J 9 2
♣ A Q J 5 3

West
♠ J
♡ Q 10 7 3
♢ Q 8 7 5 4 3
♣ K 10

East
♠ Q 9 4 2
♡ A K J 9 6 5
♢ —
♣ 7 6 2

South
♠ K 10 8 7 5 3
♡ 2
♢ A 10 6
♣ 9 8 4

With North-South 60 on score, the bidding goes:

South	West	North	East
—	—	1♣	2♡[1]
2♠	4♡[2]	pass[3]	pass
double[4]	pass	pass	pass

[1]A weak jump overcall (see page 88). The idea is to make it difficult for the opponents to get together.

[2]West doesn't expect to make Four Hearts, but at the same

time he feels certain that North-South can make nine or ten tricks in spades. He is willing to sacrifice up to the level of Four Hearts and it is good tactics to make this call immediately. Lack of BIDDING SPACE may cause the opponents to make a wrong decision.

[3]Another instructive call. North is prepared either to defend against Four Hearts or to play in Four Spades if his partner wants to bid on. His pass is not necessarily weak. As he has opened the bidding and his partner has bid at the Two level, he certainly does not propose to defend against Four Hearts *un*doubled. However, he leaves the choice of action to his partner. A pass in such a situation is called a FORCING PASS.

[4]South has a fairly close decision whether to double or bid Four Spades (which, as the cards lie, he could make). The fact that his side has a useful part score makes him decide in favor of the double. After taking the penalty he will still have 60 points below the line.

East becomes the declarer and West the dummy.

When opponents are obviously sacrificing, a trump lead, to prevent them from making their trumps separately, is often best. But here South, as leader, has a sound alternative in the suit his partner has bid.

Trick 1. South leads the 9 of clubs. Dummy plays the 10 and North the Jack.

Trick 2. Seeing the singleton spade in dummy, North judges that declarer will want to ruff some spade losers. To cut down the ruffing power, he returns a heart, which is won in dummy.

Trick 3. Declarer leads a diamond from dummy and ruffs in his hand.

Trick 4. East now leads a low spade towards the Jack. South lets this run up to North's Ace.

Trick 5. Continuing his plan to reduce dummy's trumps before declarer can ruff spades, North leads his second trump.

Against this defense, declarer can make only the six top trumps in his own hand plus two spade ruffs in dummy. He is two down doubled, losing 500. This is an honorable result for both sides. North and South might have won the rubber (620 points) in Four Spades, but they have instead gained 500 points as a penalty and still retain their 60 below the line.

A neat conclusion

The part score, as it turns out, proves of no benefit, for the rubber ends with this deal:

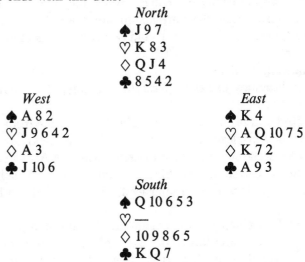

North
♠ J 9 7
♡ K 8 3
◇ Q J 4
♣ 8 5 4 2

West
♠ A 8 2
♡ J 9 6 4 2
◇ A 3
♣ J 10 6

East
♠ K 4
♡ A Q 10 7 5
◇ K 7 2
♣ A 9 3

South
♠ Q 10 6 5 3
♡ —
◇ 10 9 8 6 5
♣ K Q 7

East opens One Heart and the bidding goes:

South	West	North	East
—	—	—	1♡
pass	3♡	pass	4♣[1]
pass	4◇[2]	pass	4NT[3]
pass	5♡[4]	pass	5NT[5]
pass	6♣[6]	pass	6♡
pass	pass	pass	

[1]With first or second round controls in every suit, East is

hopeful of a slam after partner's forcing raise. As hearts are the agreed trump suit, the bid of Four Clubs shows a control, not a biddable suit.

[2]West tentatively accepts the slam suggestion by showing a control below the game level. Had he been weak for his first call he would have bid simply Four Hearts now.

[3]Blackwood convention, asking for Aces.

[4]Showing two Aces.

[5]Blackwood, asking for Kings. By bidding Five No Trump East confirms that the partnership holds all the Aces. This assurance may enable West to bid Seven if he has undisclosed strength.

[6]Showing no Kings.

East becomes declarer, West the dummy, and South the leader.

South has a probable trick in clubs, but the King from K Q x is a dangerous lead, always likely to cost a trick. Here, for example, declarer would take the King with the Ace, give up a trick to the Queen and establish a second trick in the suit. The 10 of diamonds is a much safer lead, which of itself can hardly cost a trick.

Trick 1. Declarer wins the diamond lead in dummy.

Trick 2. Declarer leads the Jack of hearts from dummy. North correctly plays low. It is often right to cover an honor with an honor, but remember that the object of doing so is to promote a lower card in partner's hand. There was no possibility of that here, and to cover with the King would only help declarer. Playing the odds, East lets the Jack of hearts run, and it holds.

Tricks 3 & 4. East now takes another heart finesse, playing the Queen from his hand, then draws the heart King with the Ace.

Tricks 5 to 7. Declarer plays King of spades, Ace of spades and ruffs a spade in his hand.

Tricks 8 and 9. East cashes the King of diamonds, then ruffs a diamond in dummy. The position is now:

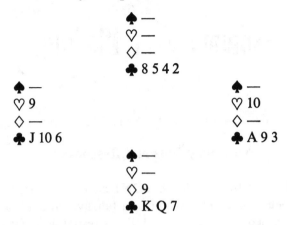

♠ —
♡ —
◇ —
♣ 8 5 4 2

♠ —   ♠ —
♡ 9   ♡ 10
◇ —   ◇ —
♣ J 10 6   ♣ A 9 3

♠ —
♡ —
◇ 9
♣ K Q 7

The lead is in dummy, and either by luck or judgment East has brought about a classic end position. He leads the Jack of clubs from dummy and lets it run to South's Queen. Now South is in a dilemma. A club return is obviously hopeless, and if he leads a diamond, declarer will be able to trump in one hand while discarding a losing club from the other. This situation, where declarer trumps in one hand and discards a loser from the other is known as a SLUFF AND RUFF. The defenders must usually try to avoid giving declarer such an opportunity, but here South has no good alternative.

The position arose as a result of declarer's clever play in eliminating the spades and diamonds from both his hands before conceding a trick in clubs. For making Six Hearts, East and West score 180 below, 750 for a vulnerable small slam, and 500 for rubber.

Summary of Bidding

The point count: 4 for Ace, 3 for King, 2 for Queen, 1 for Jack.

No Trump Bids and Responses

Open 1NT on 16 to 18. Raise to 2NT on 7 to 8. Raise to 3NT on 9. When raising, give weight to a fair five-card suit and to useful intermediates like 10's and 9's. A response of Two of a suit is weak. A response of Three of a suit is forcing. The Stayman response (Two Clubs) asks opener to bid a four-card major or, failing that, Two Diamonds.

Open 2NT on 21 to 23. Raise to Three on 4 points or a five-card suit headed by the King. A response of Three in a suit is forcing. Three Clubs can be played as Stayman, asking opener to bid a four-card major, or Three Diamonds, or Three No Trump when his only four-card suit is clubs.

Open 3NT on a balanced 25 or on less with a solid minor suit and all suits guarded. Any response is encouraging.

Opening Suit Bids

Open One of a suit on 13, or on 12 with a fair five-card suit, or 11 with a good six-card suit or two five-card suits.

Open Two of a suit, forcing to game, on very strong hands, upwards of 19 with powerful distribution. Negative response, 2NT. Any other response promises at least 5 points.

Open Three or Four of a suit on about 4 to 10 points with a long suit. Any new suit over a Three bid is forcing.

Responding to Bids of One

(It is assumed throughout this section that the responder has not previously passed)

Respond 1NT on 6 to 9; 2NT (forcing) on 13 to 14; 3NT on 15 to 16.

Respond One of a suit on 6 to 16. This is forcing for one round.

Respond Two of a lower-ranking suit on 9 to 16. This is forcing for one round.

Jump in a new suit, forcing to game, with upwards of 17, or less with exceptional support for partner's suit or a very strong suit of your own.

Raise to Two with from 3 to 10, depending on trump support and ruffing values (i.e. short suits).

Raise to Three, forcing, on upwards of 11 with four trumps and a singleton, or 13 with four trumps and a doubleton. Upper range about 15.

Raise to Four defensively on about 3 to 9 points and very good trumps and distribution.

Rebids by the Opener

(a) After a suit response at the level of One

Rebid 1NT on 13 to 16; 2NT on 18 to 20; 3NT on 21 to 22.

Minimum rebid of suit or single raise of partner's suit: limited opening, from 11 upwards.

New suit at minimum level: from a minimum up to about 19.

New suit at the Two level, higher than the first suit (a "reverse," e.g. 1 ♦-1 ♠-2♡): at least a King better than minimum.

Jump rebid of first suit: good suit and about an Ace better than a minimum opening.

Jump raise: good trump support and 14 to 19, according to distribution. Not forcing.

Jump in a new suit: forcing to game; upwards of 19, or less with strong support or powerful suits.

(b) After a suit response at the level of Two

Rebid 2NT on 15 to 17; 3NT on 18 to 20.

Minimum rebid of suit or single raise: limited opening, from 11 upwards.

New suit at minimum level: from a minimum up to about 18.

New suit at the Two level, higher than the first suit (a "reverse," e.g. 1♡-2♣-2♠): forcing, at least a King better than minimum.

Jump rebid of first suit: forcing, at least a King better than minimum.

Jump raise: good trump support and 15 to 18, according to distribution.

Jump in a new suit: forcing to game; upwards of 18, or less with strong support or powerful suits.

(c) After a response of 1NT

Bid 2NT on 17 to 18.

Bid 3NT on 19 or more.

(d) After a single raise

With balanced hand generally pass on 16, bid 2NT on 17 to 18.

With about an Ace better than a minimum opening, try for game by raising to Three, or bid a new suit, forcing for one round.

Bids by the Defending Side

Overcalls at the level of One: fair suit, from 5 to 14 not vulnerable, about 8 to 14 vulnerable.

Overcalls at the level of Two: good suit, from 8 to 14, always good playing values when vulnerable.

Jump overcalls (e.g. 2♡ over 1◇ or 3♣ over 1♠): good suit, 7 to 10 points.

Double for a takeout on most strong hands and on upwards of 11 with good distribution (i.e. singleton or void in opponent's suit and support for all other suits).

Overcall 1NT with a guard in opponent's suit and strength similar to a 1NT opening of 16 to 18.

Overcall in opponent's suit, forcing for at least two rounds, on very strong hand usually containing Ace or void in the opponent's suit.

Against opening Three bids a double is primarily for a takeout.

Index

Scoring Table

Scores above the line

Overtricks

	Not vulnerable	Vulnerable
Undoubled	Ordinary trick value	Ordinary trick value
Doubled	100 per trick	200 per trick
Redoubled	200 per trick	400 per trick

Additional bonus

For making any doubled or redoubled contract   50

Honors

4 trump honors in any one hand   100
5 trump honors in any one hand   150
At No Trump, 4 Aces in one hand   150

Slam bonuses

	Not vulnerable	Vulnerable
Small slam	500	750
Grand slam	1000	1500

Penalties for undertricks

	Not vulnerable	Vulnerable
Undoubled	50 each trick	100 each trick
Doubled	100 for first trick, 200 for each additional trick	200 for first trick, 300 for each additional trick
Redoubled	Twice the doubled penalty	Twice the doubled penalty

Rubber bonus

When the rubber is won in two games   700
When the rubber is won by two games to one   500

Unfinished rubber

     Bonus for a side with a game   300

     Bonus for a part score in an unfinished game   50

Score below the line for contracts bid and made

Spades or hearts	30 per trick
Diamonds or clubs	20 per trick
No Trump	40 for first trick, 30 for each subsequent trick

If the contract has been doubled, multiply the trick score by 2; if redoubled, by 4.

100 points below the line wins game, but no separate score is recorded until the rubber has been won.

A CATALOG OF SELECTED

DOVER BOOKS

IN ALL FIELDS OF INTEREST

A CATALOG OF SELECTED DOVER
BOOKS IN ALL FIELDS OF INTEREST

CONCERNING THE SPIRITUAL IN ART, Wassily Kandinsky. Pioneering work by father of abstract art. Thoughts on color theory, nature of art. Analysis of earlier masters. 12 illustrations. 80pp. of text. 5⅜ x 8½.   0-486-23411-8

CELTIC ART: The Methods of Construction, George Bain. Simple geometric techniques for making Celtic interlacements, spirals, Kells-type initials, animals, humans, etc. Over 500 illustrations. 160pp. 9 x 12. (Available in U.S. only.)   0-486-22923-8

AN ATLAS OF ANATOMY FOR ARTISTS, Fritz Schider. Most thorough reference work on art anatomy in the world. Hundreds of illustrations, including selections from works by Vesalius, Leonardo, Goya, Ingres, Michelangelo, others. 593 illustrations. 192pp. 7⅞ x 10¼.   0-486-20241-0

CELTIC HAND STROKE-BY-STROKE (Irish Half-Uncial from "The Book of Kells"): An Arthur Baker Calligraphy Manual, Arthur Baker. Complete guide to creating each letter of the alphabet in distinctive Celtic manner. Covers hand position, strokes, pens, inks, paper, more. Illustrated. 48pp. 8¼ x 11.   0-486-24336-2

EASY ORIGAMI, John Montroll. Charming collection of 32 projects (hat, cup, pelican, piano, swan, many more) specially designed for the novice origami hobbyist. Clearly illustrated easy-to-follow instructions insure that even beginning papercrafters will achieve successful results. 48pp. 8¼ x 11.   0-486-27298-2

BLOOMINGDALE'S ILLUSTRATED 1886 CATALOG: Fashions, Dry Goods and Housewares, Bloomingdale Brothers. Famed merchants' extremely rare catalog depicting about 1,700 products: clothing, housewares, firearms, dry goods, jewelry, more. Invaluable for dating, identifying vintage items. Also, copyright-free graphics for artists, designers. Co-published with Henry Ford Museum & Greenfield Village. 160pp. 8¼ x 11.   0-486-25780-0

THE ART OF WORLDLY WISDOM, Baltasar Gracian. "Think with the few and speak with the many," "Friends are a second existence," and "Be able to forget" are among this 1637 volume's 300 pithy maxims. A perfect source of mental and spiritual refreshment, it can be opened at random and appreciated either in brief or at length. 128pp. 5⅜ x 8½.   0-486-44034-6

JOHNSON'S DICTIONARY: A Modern Selection, Samuel Johnson (E. L. McAdam and George Milne, eds.). This modern version reduces the original 1755 edition's 2,300 pages of definitions and literary examples to a more manageable length, retaining the verbal pleasure and historical curiosity of the original. 480pp. 5³⁄₁₆ x 8¼.   0-486-44089-3

ADVENTURES OF HUCKLEBERRY FINN, Mark Twain, Illustrated by E. W. Kemble. A work of eternal richness and complexity, a source of ongoing critical debate, and a literary landmark, Twain's 1885 masterpiece about a barefoot boy's journey of self-discovery has enthralled readers around the world. This handsome clothbound reproduction of the first edition features all 174 of the original black-and-white illustrations. 368pp. 5⅜ x 8½.   0-486-44322-1

FRENCH STORIES/CONTES FRANÇAIS: A Dual-Language Book, Wallace Fowlie. Ten stories by French masters, Voltaire to Camus: "Micromegas" by Voltaire; "The Atheist's Mass" by Balzac; "Minuet" by de Maupassant; "The Guest" by Camus, six more. Excellent English translations on facing pages. Also French-English vocabulary list, exercises, more. 352pp. 5⅜ x 8½. 0-486-26443-2

CHICAGO AT THE TURN OF THE CENTURY IN PHOTOGRAPHS: 122 Historic Views from the Collections of the Chicago Historical Society, Larry A. Viskochil. Rare large-format prints offer detailed views of City Hall, State Street, the Loop, Hull House, Union Station, many other landmarks, circa 1904-1913. Introduction. Captions. Maps. 144pp. 9⅜ x 12¼. 0-486-24656-6

OLD BROOKLYN IN EARLY PHOTOGRAPHS, 1865-1929, William Lee Younger. Luna Park, Gravesend race track, construction of Grand Army Plaza, moving of Hotel Brighton, etc. 157 previously unpublished photographs. 165pp. 8⅞ x 11¾. 0-486-23587-4

THE MYTHS OF THE NORTH AMERICAN INDIANS, Lewis Spence. Rich anthology of the myths and legends of the Algonquins, Iroquois, Pawnees and Sioux, prefaced by an extensive historical and ethnological commentary. 36 illustrations. 480pp. 5⅜ x 8½. 0-486-25967-6

AN ENCYCLOPEDIA OF BATTLES: Accounts of Over 1,560 Battles from 1479 B.C. to the Present, David Eggenberger. Essential details of every major battle in recorded history from the first battle of Megiddo in 1479 B.C. to Grenada in 1984. List of Battle Maps. New Appendix covering the years 1967-1984. Index. 99 illustrations. 544pp. 6½ x 9¼. 0-486-24913-1

SAILING ALONE AROUND THE WORLD, Captain Joshua Slocum. First man to sail around the world, alone, in small boat. One of great feats of seamanship told in delightful manner. 67 illustrations. 294pp. 5⅜ x 8½. 0-486-20326-3

ANARCHISM AND OTHER ESSAYS, Emma Goldman. Powerful, penetrating, prophetic essays on direct action, role of minorities, prison reform, puritan hypocrisy, violence, etc. 271pp. 5⅜ x 8½. 0-486-22484-8

MYTHS OF THE HINDUS AND BUDDHISTS, Ananda K. Coomaraswamy and Sister Nivedita. Great stories of the epics; deeds of Krishna, Shiva, taken from puranas, Vedas, folk tales; etc. 32 illustrations. 400pp. 5⅜ x 8½. 0-486-21759-0

MY BONDAGE AND MY FREEDOM, Frederick Douglass. Born a slave, Douglass became outspoken force in antislavery movement. The best of Douglass' autobiographies. Graphic description of slave life. 464pp. 5⅜ x 8½. 0-486-22457-0

FOLLOWING THE EQUATOR: A Journey Around the World, Mark Twain. Fascinating humorous account of 1897 voyage to Hawaii, Australia, India, New Zealand, etc. Ironic, bemused reports on peoples, customs, climate, flora and fauna, politics, much more. 197 illustrations. 720pp. 5⅜ x 8½. 0-486-26113-1

THE PEOPLE CALLED SHAKERS, Edward D. Andrews. Definitive study of Shakers: origins, beliefs, practices, dances, social organization, furniture and crafts, etc. 33 illustrations. 351pp. 5⅜ x 8½. 0-486-21081-2

THE MYTHS OF GREECE AND ROME, H. A. Guerber. A classic of mythology, generously illustrated, long prized for its simple, graphic, accurate retelling of the principal myths of Greece and Rome, and for its commentary on their origins and significance. With 64 illustrations by Michelangelo, Raphael, Titian, Rubens, Canova, Bernini and others. 480pp. 5⅜ x 8½. 0-486-27584-1

HOW TO DO BEADWORK, Mary White. Fundamental book on craft from simple projects to five-bead chains and woven works. 106 illustrations. 142pp. 5⅜ x 8.
0-486-20697-1

THE 1912 AND 1915 GUSTAV STICKLEY FURNITURE CATALOGS, Gustav Stickley. With over 200 detailed illustrations and descriptions, these two catalogs are essential reading and reference materials and identification guides for Stickley furniture. Captions cite materials, dimensions and prices. 112pp. 6½ x 9¼. 0-486-26676-1

EARLY AMERICAN LOCOMOTIVES, John H. White, Jr. Finest locomotive engravings from early 19th century: historical (1804–74), main-line (after 1870), special, foreign, etc. 147 plates. 142pp. 11⅜ x 8¼. 0-486-22772-3

LITTLE BOOK OF EARLY AMERICAN CRAFTS AND TRADES, Peter Stockham (ed.). 1807 children's book explains crafts and trades: baker, hatter, cooper, potter, and many others. 23 copperplate illustrations. 140pp. 4⅝/8 x 6.
0-486-23336-7

VICTORIAN FASHIONS AND COSTUMES FROM HARPER'S BAZAR, 1867–1898, Stella Blum (ed.). Day costumes, evening wear, sports clothes, shoes, hats, other accessories in over 1,000 detailed engravings. 320pp. 9⅜ x 12¼.
0-486-22990-4

THE LONG ISLAND RAIL ROAD IN EARLY PHOTOGRAPHS, Ron Ziel. Over 220 rare photos, informative text document origin (1844) and development of rail service on Long Island. Vintage views of early trains, locomotives, stations, passengers, crews, much more. Captions. 8⅞ x 11¾. 0-486-26301-0

VOYAGE OF THE LIBERDADE, Joshua Slocum. Great 19th-century mariner's thrilling, first-hand account of the wreck of his ship off South America, the 35-foot boat he built from the wreckage, and its remarkable voyage home. 128pp. 5⅜ x 8½.
0-486-40022-0

TEN BOOKS ON ARCHITECTURE, Vitruvius. The most important book ever written on architecture. Early Roman aesthetics, technology, classical orders, site selection, all other aspects. Morgan translation. 331pp. 5⅜ x 8½. 0-486-20645-9

THE HUMAN FIGURE IN MOTION, Eadweard Muybridge. More than 4,500 stopped-action photos, in action series, showing undraped men, women, children jumping, lying down, throwing, sitting, wrestling, carrying, etc. 390pp. 7⅞ x 10⅝.
0-486-20204-6 Clothbd.

TREES OF THE EASTERN AND CENTRAL UNITED STATES AND CANADA, William M. Harlow. Best one-volume guide to 140 trees. Full descriptions, woodlore, range, etc. Over 600 illustrations. Handy size. 288pp. 4½ x 6⅜. 0-486-20395-6

GROWING AND USING HERBS AND SPICES, Milo Miloradovich. Versatile handbook provides all the information needed for cultivation and use of all the herbs and spices available in North America. 4 illustrations. Index. Glossary. 236pp. 5⅜ x 8½.
0-486-25058-X

BIG BOOK OF MAZES AND LABYRINTHS, Walter Shepherd. 50 mazes and labyrinths in all—classical, solid, ripple, and more—in one great volume. Perfect inexpensive puzzler for clever youngsters. Full solutions. 112pp. 8⅛ x 11. 0-486-22951-3

PIANO TUNING, J. Cree Fischer. Clearest, best book for beginner, amateur. Simple repairs, raising dropped notes, tuning by easy method of flattened fifths. No previous skills needed. 4 illustrations. 201pp. 5⅜ x 8½. 0-486-23267-0

HINTS TO SINGERS, Lillian Nordica. Selecting the right teacher, developing confidence, overcoming stage fright, and many other important skills receive thoughtful discussion in this indispensible guide, written by a world-famous diva of four decades' experience. 96pp. 5⅜ x 8½. 0-486-40094-8

THE COMPLETE NONSENSE OF EDWARD LEAR, Edward Lear. All nonsense limericks, zany alphabets, Owl and Pussycat, songs, nonsense botany, etc., illustrated by Lear. Total of 320pp. 5⅜ x 8½. (Available in U.S. only.) 0-486-20167-8

VICTORIAN PARLOUR POETRY: An Annotated Anthology, Michael R. Turner. 117 gems by Longfellow, Tennyson, Browning, many lesser-known poets. "The Village Blacksmith," "Curfew Must Not Ring Tonight," "Only a Baby Small," dozens more, often difficult to find elsewhere. Index of poets, titles, first lines. xxiii + 325pp. 5⅝ x 8¼. 0-486-27044-0

DUBLINERS, James Joyce. Fifteen stories offer vivid, tightly focused observations of the lives of Dublin's poorer classes. At least one, "The Dead," is considered a masterpiece. Reprinted complete and unabridged from standard edition. 160pp. 5$\frac{3}{16}$ x 8¼. 0-486-26870-5

GREAT WEIRD TALES: 14 Stories by Lovecraft, Blackwood, Machen and Others, S. T. Joshi (ed.). 14 spellbinding tales, including "The Sin Eater," by Fiona McLeod, "The Eye Above the Mantel," by Frank Belknap Long, as well as renowned works by R. H. Barlow, Lord Dunsany, Arthur Machen, W. C. Morrow and eight other masters of the genre. 256pp. 5⅜ x 8½. (Available in U.S. only.) 0-486-40436-6

THE BOOK OF THE SACRED MAGIC OF ABRAMELIN THE MAGE, translated by S. MacGregor Mathers. Medieval manuscript of ceremonial magic. Basic document in Aleister Crowley, Golden Dawn groups. 268pp. 5⅜ x 8½. 0-486-23211-5

THE BATTLES THAT CHANGED HISTORY, Fletcher Pratt. Eminent historian profiles 16 crucial conflicts, ancient to modern, that changed the course of civilization. 352pp. 5⅜ x 8½. 0-486-41129-X

NEW RUSSIAN-ENGLISH AND ENGLISH-RUSSIAN DICTIONARY, M. A. O'Brien. This is a remarkably handy Russian dictionary, containing a surprising amount of information, including over 70,000 entries. 366pp. 4½ x 6⅛. 0-486-20208-9

NEW YORK IN THE FORTIES, Andreas Feininger. 162 brilliant photographs by the well-known photographer, formerly with *Life* magazine. Commuters, shoppers, Times Square at night, much else from city at its peak. Captions by John von Hartz. 181pp. 9¼ x 10¾. 0-486-23585-8

INDIAN SIGN LANGUAGE, William Tomkins. Over 525 signs developed by Sioux and other tribes. Written instructions and diagrams. Also 290 pictographs. 111pp. 6⅛ x 9¼. 0-486-22029-X

ANATOMY: A Complete Guide for Artists, Joseph Sheppard. A master of figure drawing shows artists how to render human anatomy convincingly. Over 460 illustrations. 224pp. 8⅜ x 11¼. 0-486-27279-6

MEDIEVAL CALLIGRAPHY: Its History and Technique, Marc Drogin. Spirited history, comprehensive instruction manual covers 13 styles (ca. 4th century through 15th). Excellent photographs; directions for duplicating medieval techniques with modern tools. 224pp. 8⅜ x 11¼. 0-486-26142-5

DRIED FLOWERS: How to Prepare Them, Sarah Whitlock and Martha Rankin. Complete instructions on how to use silica gel, meal and borax, perlite aggregate, sand and borax, glycerine and water to create attractive permanent flower arrangements. 12 illustrations. 32pp. 5⅜ x 8½. 0-486-21802-3

EASY-TO-MAKE BIRD FEEDERS FOR WOODWORKERS, Scott D. Campbell. Detailed, simple-to-use guide for designing, constructing, caring for and using feeders. Text, illustrations for 12 classic and contemporary designs. 96pp. 5⅜ x 8½. 0-486-25847-5

THE COMPLETE BOOK OF BIRDHOUSE CONSTRUCTION FOR WOOD-WORKERS, Scott D. Campbell. Detailed instructions, illustrations, tables. Also data on bird habitat and instinct patterns. Bibliography. 3 tables. 63 illustrations in 15 figures. 48pp. 5¼ x 8½. 0-486-24407-5

SCOTTISH WONDER TALES FROM MYTH AND LEGEND, Donald A. Mackenzie. 16 lively tales tell of giants rumbling down mountainsides, of a magic wand that turns stone pillars into warriors, of gods and goddesses, evil hags, powerful forces and more. 240pp. 5⅜ x 8½. 0-486-29677-6

THE HISTORY OF UNDERCLOTHES, C. Willett Cunnington and Phyllis Cunnington. Fascinating, well-documented survey covering six centuries of English undergarments, enhanced with over 100 illustrations: 12th-century laced-up bodice, footed long drawers (1795), 19th-century bustles, l9th-century corsets for men, Victorian "bust improvers," much more. 272pp. 5⅜ x 8¼. 0-486-27124-2

ARTS AND CRAFTS FURNITURE: The Complete Brooks Catalog of 1912, Brooks Manufacturing Co. Photos and detailed descriptions of more than 150 now very collectible furniture designs from the Arts and Crafts movement depict davenports, settees, buffets, desks, tables, chairs, bedsteads, dressers and more, all built of solid, quarter-sawed oak. Invaluable for students and enthusiasts of antiques, Americana and the decorative arts. 80pp. 6½ x 9¼. 0-486-27471-3

WILBUR AND ORVILLE: A Biography of the Wright Brothers, Fred Howard. Definitive, crisply written study tells the full story of the brothers' lives and work. A vividly written biography, unparalleled in scope and color, that also captures the spirit of an extraordinary era. 560pp. 6⅛ x 9¼. 0-486-40297-5

THE ARTS OF THE SAILOR: Knotting, Splicing and Ropework, Hervey Garrett Smith. Indispensable shipboard reference covers tools, basic knots and useful hitches; handsewing and canvas work, more. Over 100 illustrations. Delightful reading for sea lovers. 256pp. 5⅜ x 8½. 0-486-26440-8

FRANK LLOYD WRIGHT'S FALLINGWATER: The House and Its History, Second, Revised Edition, Donald Hoffmann. A total revision–both in text and illustrations–of the standard document on Fallingwater, the boldest, most personal architectural statement of Wright's mature years, updated with valuable new material from the recently opened Frank Lloyd Wright Archives. "Fascinating"–*The New York Times*. 116 illustrations. 128pp. 9¼ x 10¾. 0-486-27430-6

PHOTOGRAPHIC SKETCHBOOK OF THE CIVIL WAR, Alexander Gardner. 100 photos taken on field during the Civil War. Famous shots of Manassas Harper's Ferry, Lincoln, Richmond, slave pens, etc. 244pp. 10⅝ x 8¼. 0-486-22731-6

FIVE ACRES AND INDEPENDENCE, Maurice G. Kains. Great back-to-the-land classic explains basics of self-sufficient farming. The one book to get. 95 illustrations. 397pp. 5⅜ x 8½. 0-486-20974-1

CATALOG OF DOVER BOOKS

LIGHT AND SHADE: A Classic Approach to Three-Dimensional Drawing, Mrs. Mary P. Merrifield. Handy reference clearly demonstrates principles of light and shade by revealing effects of common daylight, sunshine, and candle or artificial light on geometrical solids. 13 plates. 64pp. 5$\frac{3}{8}$ x 8$\frac{1}{2}$. 0-486-44143-1

ASTROLOGY AND ASTRONOMY: A Pictorial Archive of Signs and Symbols, Ernst and Johanna Lehner. Treasure trove of stories, lore, and myth, accompanied by more than 300 rare illustrations of planets, the Milky Way, signs of the zodiac, comets, meteors, and other astronomical phenomena. 192pp. 8$\frac{3}{8}$ x 11. 0-486-43981-X

JEWELRY MAKING: Techniques for Metal, Tim McCreight. Easy-to-follow instructions and carefully executed illustrations describe tools and techniques, use of gems and enamels, wire inlay, casting, and other topics. 72 line illustrations and diagrams. 176pp. 8$\frac{1}{4}$ x 10$\frac{7}{8}$. 0-486-44043-5

MAKING BIRDHOUSES: Easy and Advanced Projects, Gladstone Califf. Easy-to-follow instructions include diagrams for everything from a one-room house for bluebirds to a forty-two-room structure for purple martins. 56 plates; 4 figures. 80pp. 8$\frac{3}{4}$ x 6$\frac{3}{8}$. 0-486-44183-0

LITTLE BOOK OF LOG CABINS: How to Build and Furnish Them, William S. Wicks. Handy how-to manual, with instructions and illustrations for building cabins in the Adirondack style, fireplaces, stairways, furniture, beamed ceilings, and more. 102 line drawings. 96pp. 8$\frac{3}{4}$ x 6$\frac{3}{8}$. 0-486-44259-4

THE SEASONS OF AMERICA PAST, Eric Sloane. From "sugaring time" and strawberry picking to Indian summer and fall harvest, a whole year's activities described in charming prose and enhanced with 79 of the author's own illustrations. 160pp. 8$\frac{1}{4}$ x 11. 0-486-44220-9

THE METROPOLIS OF TOMORROW, Hugh Ferriss. Generous, prophetic vision of the metropolis of the future, as perceived in 1929. Powerful illustrations of towering structures, wide avenues, and rooftop parks–all features in many of today's modern cities. 59 illustrations. 144pp. 8$\frac{1}{4}$ x 11. 0-486-43727-2

THE PATH TO ROME, Hilaire Belloc. This 1902 memoir abounds in lively vignettes from a vanished time, recounting a pilgrimage on foot across the Alps and Apennines in order to "see all Europe which the Christian Faith has saved." 77 of the author's original line drawings complement his sparkling prose. 272pp. 5$\frac{3}{8}$ x 8$\frac{1}{2}$. 0-486-44001-X

THE HISTORY OF RASSELAS: Prince of Abissinia, Samuel Johnson. Distinguished English writer attacks eighteenth-century optimism and man's unrealistic estimates of what life has to offer. 112pp. 5$\frac{3}{8}$ x 8$\frac{1}{2}$. 0-486-44094-X

A VOYAGE TO ARCTURUS, David Lindsay. A brilliant flight of pure fancy, where wild creatures crowd the fantastic landscape and demented torturers dominate victims with their bizarre mental powers. 272pp. 5$\frac{3}{8}$ x 8$\frac{1}{2}$. 0-486-44198-9

Paperbound unless otherwise indicated. Available at your book dealer, online at **www.doverpublications.com**, or by writing to Dept. GI, Dover Publications, Inc., 31 East 2nd Street, Mineola, NY 11501. For current price information or for free catalogs (please indicate field of interest), write to Dover Publications or log on to **www.doverpublications.com** and see every Dover book in print. Dover publishes more than 500 books each year on science, elementary and advanced mathematics, biology, music, art, literary history, social sciences, and other areas.